The Persistent Other: Strangers and Neighbors

by John Cavanaugh-O'Keefe

Section II of *McGivney's Guests*

Credits

Cover: *Hospitality of Abraham*. Based on Andrei Rublev's *Trinity*. For the icon not veiled by a persistent stranger, see: http://ssje.org/ssje/2013/01/29/andrei-rublev-br-curtis-almquist/.
copyright info: see http://creativecommons.org/licenses/by-nc-nd/3.0/deed.en_US .

Scripture texts in this work are taken from the *New American Bible*, revised edition© 2010, 1991, 1986, 1970 Confraternity of Christian Doctrine, Washington, D.C. and are used by permission of the copyright owner. All Rights Reserved. No part of the *New American Bible* may be reproduced in any form without permission in writing from the copyright owner.

ISBN-13: 978-1533115607
ISBN-10: 1533115605

© 2016 John Cavanaugh-O'Keefe

+ + + + + + +

Part II of *McGivney's Guests*

McGivney's Guests is a work in progress (2016) exploring immigration and the Knights of Columbus (KOC). The KOC is a Catholic fraternal and service organization, founded in 1882 in Connecticut by Fr. Michael J. McGivney, to serve the poor – at that time, mostly immigrants.

The whole work of which this volume is a part explores the rich teaching in Scripture and Tradition, the American experience, the extraordinary document "Strangers No Longer" written jointly by the American and Mexican bishops in 2003, and the experience of the Knights of Columbus throughout the past century.

The previous volume, *21 Stranger Claims in the Old Testament*, starts with the words of Jesus describing the Last Judgment: "Whatever you did for one of these least brothers of mine, you did for me." Jesus listed six groups of people in need, including "strangers." Why are strangers in that remarkable list? To explain why, *21 Stranger Claims* backs up to review the rich and forceful but often overlooked teaching of the Old Testament.

The Persistent Other: Strangers and Neighbors is the second section of *McGivney's Guests*. It shows the continuity of teaching about hospitality from the Old Testament into the New Testament. But it shifts from proving a point to using a light: once we understand that we can and should watch for insights about hospitality, what do we learn?

The book grew out of conversations among KOC members, and it is written by and for members – and other intelligent people. However, it is not an official publication of the Knights of Columbus.

+ + + + + + +

Apologia

Hypocrisy makes me puke. Which is a problem.

That man is a thief who in order to deceive his hearers pretends to reverence divine principles. Although he has not come to know the true quality of these principles through his actions, he traffics in glory merely by speaking about it, hoping that in this manner he will be thought righteous by his hearers and so capture their admiration. To put it simply, he whose way of life does not match his speech, and whose inner disposition is opposed to spiritual knowledge, is a thief whose appropriation of what is not his proves him to be evil. Scripture fittingly addresses these words to him: "But to the wicked God says, 'Why do you speak of my statutes and appropriate my covenant with your mouth?'" (Psalm 50: 16)

That man also is a thief who conceals his soul's unseen evil behind a seemingly virtuous way of life, and disguises his inner disposition with an affected innocence. Just as one kind of thief filches his audience's mind by uttering words of wisdom, so this kind pilfers the senses of those who see him by his pretense of virtue. To him it will be said, "Be ashamed of yourselves, all you who are dressed in clothes that do not belong to you" (Zeph 1:8), and "In that day, the Lord will reveal their pretense." I seem to hear the Lord saying these things to me daily in the hidden workshop of my heart, and I feel that I am explicitly condemned on both counts.

From *The Philokalia: Complete Text, Volume Two*. Edited by G.E.H. Palmer, Philip Sherrard, Kallistos Ware; published in London by Faber and Faber, Ltd, in 1981.

This confession and these words are from St. Maximos the Confessor. I make them my own.

Contents

Introduction: Through the lens of hospitality 6

Continuity: Old Testament to the New Testament 7

Chapter 1: Review 21 Claims 8

Chapter 2: Diction issues 15

Chapter 3: Stranger in his own land 19

Chapter 4: Good news for all nations 23

Transition point: From argument to application 31

Chapter 5: Angels and strangers (Matthew) 33

Chapter 6: Mary's story of the birth (Luke) 38

Chapter 7: Glory, grace and truth (John) 45

Chapter 8: Temptation in the desert 52

Chapter 9: The Lamb of God 55

Chapter 10: Galilee of the Gentiles 57

Chapter 11: Educating three leaders 59

Chapter 12: Hospitality in John's signs 62

Chapter 13: Hospitality smorgasbord (Luke) 66

Aside: Thomas Aquinas on washing feet 75

Chapter 14: First Feast and Last Supper 76

Chapter 15: Hospitality and the Trinity 78

Chapter 16: Hospitality in the Eucharist 82

Chapter 17: The Last Judgment (Mt 25) 86

Chapter 18: Hospitality after the Resurrection 91

Chapter 19: Hospitality fills our prayer 96

Chapter 20: Beacon on a hill 104

Introduction: Through the lens of hospitality

It is emphatically not my intention to give a complete exegesis of the New Testament, not even of one single little passage. My intention is simply to show that when we look at familiar and rich and complex passages *through the lens of hospitality*, our perception is deepened and enriched. Hospitality is a ray of light and warmth emerging from the depths of God's heart.

The first chapters of this book include some argument. Writing about the Old Testament, I argued that the theme of hospitality to strangers runs right through the whole Hebrew Bible – the Law and the Prophets and the history books and the wisdom books, from Abraham to Zechariah, from Genesis to Malachi. The current book starts out asserting firmly and with argumentative detail that there is undeniable continuity from the Old Testament to the New, with regard to hospitality. But after a few chapters on continuity, the burden of the book shifts from proving that there is a ray of light, to using that light. Assuming that hospitality is there – assuming that the point has been proven – what do we see?

In exploring what the Lord taught about hospitality, I have tried hard not to try too hard – that is, not to force the text. I do indeed want to prove a point, but am I cherry-picking the text? In *21 Stranger Claims in the Old Testament*, I tried to avoid taking lines out of context; and in this book, I am still committed to an honest reading of the text. But after chapter 4, I am less careful about separating what can be proven from what I find to be challenging or insightful or inspiring.

Another word about what I am not doing. (There are a million things I'm not doing!) I sense that there's a gaping hole in thought here, as if I have written about the Joyful and Sorrowful Mysteries, but not the Glorious. There's almost nothing in this volume about sacrifice. Scripture is an introduction to the mind of the Creator, so everything in creation is relevant, and – surprise! – I'm not talking about all of it. I'm just exploring a single ray of light – a ray that shines forth from the brilliant depths of the heart of God – but a single ray. But more pointedly, I do refer repeatedly to a pair of complementary realities, hospitality and salvation. I am uncomfortably aware that everything I say about either of them, and more especially about the two together, would be much clearer if I understood sacrifice better. What can I say? Next year, in Jerusalem. I'm one pilgrim, sharing what I do see, not what I don't.

Continuity: Old Testament to the New Testament

The first part of the book is four argumentative chapters.

Is the abundant teaching about welcoming strangers in the Old Testament carried over into the New Testament? Emphatically yes, but it takes a little explanation. To defend the claim of continuity, there are three steps.

First, I'll review the claims from 21 Stranger Claims in the Old Testament, *and indicate how they re-appear in the New Testament. Of the 21 claims, 18 have a clear echo in the New Testament, and three do not. So the list of 21 does indeed carry over from the Old Testament to the New – which you would expect if indeed hospitality is fundamental, even if it is much neglected in our time.*

Second, I'll explore the teaching about hospitality associated with the specific words for "stranger" – briefly. The extraordinary Hebrew word ger *does not have a Greek equivalent, so one convenient search tool – namely, finding relevant passages about hospitality by searching a concordance for a word – does not work as well in the New Testament as it did in the Old Testament.*

Third, I explore the differences regarding strangers in Israel, in different historical circumstances. The fundamental idea doesn't change: God sometimes reveals himself as Other, and often as a stranger; so we cannot reject strangers and welcome God. However, the way we welcome strangers can change depending on political and social circumstances. A nation committed to following God's law is – as a nation – more welcoming of strangers than a nation under foreign occupation. But if the nation drops this responsibility, God's people pick it up.

After showing the clear continuity from Old to New, I have trusted that the teaching is there, and explored what can be seen in the light of this brilliant ray. So some of the connections that I put forward, beginning with the observations on the nativity narratives, are admittedly plausible but unproven. *I have tried to show patterns. I am quite sure the patterns are solid and real, but I may have misunderstood details in various passages.*

Chapter 1: Review 21 Claims

In the first volume of this series, I said that the teaching about God's special concern for strangers is rich and abundant and clear throughout the Old Testament. To explain this, I collected and explained 21 claims that might be a little startling to many people, but were easy to verify. If these claims about God's particular care for strangers – pilgrims, immigrants, visitors – were genuine, then the same things should show up in the New Testament. Do they?

Here are the claims from the Old Testament, with remarks about teaching in the New Testament.

> 1. *Hospitality is fundamental in Biblical teaching, beginning with Abraham in Genesis: the stranger at the door should be welcomed as God. (Genesis 18)*

I started out to understand the teaching about hospitality in the Old Testament because I saw so much disagreement about what Jesus meant when he spoke about strangers in his description of the Last Judgment: "I was [hungry, thirsty ...] a stranger and you welcomed me ... Then the righteous will answer him and say, 'Lord, when did we see you a stranger and welcome you?' ... And the king will say to them in reply, 'Amen, I say to you, whatever you did for one of these least brothers of mine, you did for me.' Then he will say to those on his left, 'Depart from me, you accursed, into the eternal fire prepared for the devil and his angels. For I was [hungry, thirsty ...] a stranger and you gave me no welcome ...' Then they will answer and say, 'Lord, when did we see [hungry, thirsty ...] a stranger, and not minister to your needs?' He will answer them, 'Amen, I say to you, what you did not do for one of these least ones, you did not do for me.' And these will go off to eternal punishment, but the righteous to eternal life." (Mt 25:35-46) The teaching about welcoming strangers as God is much clearer and stronger in this passage in the New Testament than anywhere in the Old. You need the Old Testament context to be confident that you understand what a "stranger" is. But for sure, the teaching is there in the New Testament, with fire.

This key idea is also found in a neat and tidy aphorism in Hebrews 13:2: "Do not neglect hospitality, for through it some have unknowingly entertained angels."

> 2. *The story of Sodom explains that failing to welcome a stranger is deeply wrong, and is punished severely. (Gen 19)*

See above. Jesus is uncharacteristically stern about this matter: "Depart from me, you accursed, into the eternal fire prepared for the devil and his angels." Severity for a sin of omission? For sure, what happened at Sodom is still relevant in the New Testament.

> 3. *The teaching in Scripture about hospitality is often obscured by arguments about homosexuality, but you can (and should) get past that! (Genesis 18-19)*

The issue here is not so much about whether the teaching about hospitality is there in Scripture, specifically in the story of Sodom, but how this teaching is obscured in later teaching. That danger of confusion is definitely still there in the New Testament. No one in the Old Testament used the story of Sodom to refer to sexual sins. Instead, three prophets used Sodom as a byword for injustice, for flaunting luxury in the face of the poor, for arrogance. In the New Testament, both Matthew and Luke use Sodom referring to inhospitality, without any hint of sexual sin. But two Epistles – First Peter and Jude – refer to Sodom to denounce homosexual acts, without any hint of inhospitality. So this challenge, this possibility of confusion, is in the New Testament, not the Old.

> 4. *The theme of hospitality in the story of Mamre and Sodom illuminates the Last Supper.*
> 5. *The theme of hospitality from Genesis through the Gospels can be obscured by a truly weird competition, setting sacrifice against hospitality.*
> 6. *Jesus holds up Abraham as a symbol of wealth used properly – that is, hospitably – contrasted with Dives,*

> *whose abuse of wealth – that is, whose inhospitality – was damnable.*

These three were remarks about the New and Old together: there's no need to explain whether they are still relevant in the New Testament.

> 7. *Moses did not describe the evil of Egypt as genocide or treachery, but as inhospitality. Welcome strangers, because – remember! – you too once were a stranger in a strange land. (Exodus)*

This key idea in the teaching of Moses is indeed affirmed in the New Testament, but the transition requires some explanation. In brief: what Moses said about strangers is taken up in what Jesus says about neighbors. Both asked us to put ourselves in the place of people and need. Moses: Welcome strangers because – remember! – you too were once a stranger in a strange land. Jesus: Who was neighbor to the victim left by the side of the road?

> 8. *Undergirding the 613 rules in the Law of Moses, there are several principles; one foundational principle is hospitality. (Leviticus)*

Jesus sums up the whole Law in two commandments. The first is, love God with your whole heart and soul and mind and strength; this is the greatest commandment. The second is like it: love your neighbor as yourself. Together, these two sum up the whole law, says Jesus. (Mt 22:36-40) But pressed for a little clarity about these two commandments (in Luke's Gospel), Jesus explains what he means by love of neighbor using the parable of the Good Samaritan, a story about hospitality to a stranger. In Leviticus, a handful of laws are explained by reference to hospitality; in Luke, Jesus explains the second of the two great commandments by reference to hospitality.

> 9. *The principles that undergird the law have a tone that is different from the rules, a tone of tender care – and hospitality. (Leviticus)*

The fascinating shifts in tone found in Leviticus are standard throughout the Gospels. Repeatedly, Jesus responds to small questions – often trick questions about legal interpretations – with stories that are directly responsive but that shift the conversation to far larger issues. This happens over and over with questions about observing the Sabbath. But it also comes up in other contexts, including the story of the woman at the well (John 4) – a complex story about repentance and prayer and forgiveness, but also about thirst and hospitality.

> 10. *God demands equality between native-born and immigrants. There are a few exceptions to strict equality (e.g., road kill rules); but almost all exceptions favor immigrants, the "preferential option for the poor." (Leviticus)*

In Palestine under occupation, and then during the diaspora of the early Church, the distinctions between native-born Jews and immigrants was not a pressing issue. But navigating the differences between Jews and Greeks was fundamental in the work and teaching of the early Church, especially Paul's missionary activity. See, for example, Galatians 3:28: "There is neither Jew nor Greek, there is neither slave nor free person, there is not male and female; for you are all one in Christ Jesus." The first council of the Church is recorded in Acts (chapter 15), and it was held to discuss this issue. Peter's remark gets to the heart of the issue: "And God, who knows the heart, bore witness by granting them [non-Jews] the Holy Spirit just as he did us [Jews]. He made no distinction between us and them, for by faith he purified their hearts." (Acts 15: 8-9)

> 11. *The principle of hospitality is, arguably, more fundamental than the Ten Commandments. (Deuteronomy)*

See #8 above.

> 12. *The story of Gibea clarifies the story of Sodom. It relates the third (of four: Sodom, Egypt, Gibea, Babylon)*

> *extraordinarily severe punishment for violating hospitality. (Judges)*

The story of the incarnation, as told is John, can be seen as another story of inhospitality by an entire society. The punishment for this incredible crime of inhospitality is crucifixion, and Jesus takes the punishment on himself. (More below; see chapter 7.)

> 13. *The delightful story of Ruth establishes David's credentials as part-stranger. Abraham, Moses, Elijah, David, and Jesus – Patriarch, Law-Giver, Prophet, King, and Messiah – all experienced the life of a stranger. (Ruth)*

This is about the New and Old together: there's no need to explain whether it is still relevant in the New Testament.

> 14. *The prophets, including Elijah, demand special care for widows and orphans – and strangers. Throughout Scripture, there is a familiar trio, not just a familiar pair. (1 Kings)*

Oddly, special concern for the widow/orphan pair is almost gone in the New Testament, but the special concern for strangers persists; see especially the list in Matthew 25 of people who should receive preferential treatment.

> 15. *Job defends himself, explaining that he was a just man. A key point in this defense: he was hospitable to strangers. (Job)*

There is no clear echo in the New Testament of these words of Job's. There is a place where it would might been appropriate to use them, had Jesus or the author of the Gospel chosen to do so; but they did not. The disciples of John the Baptist ask Jesus if he is the one who is to come, and Jesus lists the signs he has performed: "the blind regain their sight, the lame walk, lepers are cleansed, the deaf hear, the dead are raised, and the poor have the good news proclaimed to them." (Mt 11:5 and Lk 7:20) He does not say anything about caring for strangers.

Perhaps Jesus and his followers do not express a specific concern for strangers because they have become strangers themselves. See, for example, what Jesus said to one man who stated his intention to follow Jesus: ""Foxes have dens and birds of the sky have nests, but the Son of Man has nowhere to rest his head." (Mt 8:20 and Lk 9:58)

> 16. *Here on God's earth, we all have the status of strangers. (Psalm 39)*

This is echoed in John's description of the incarnation, in the mission work of all the disciples of Jesus, and throughout the missionary work of Paul – to mention a few.

The idea of being strangers and exiles here on earth is echoed clearly in Hebrews: "All these [Abraham and his descendants] died in faith. They did not receive what had been promised but saw it and greeted it from afar and acknowledged themselves to be strangers and aliens on earth, for those who speak thus show that they are seeking a homeland." (Hebrews 11:13-14)

> 17. *Abusing strangers is repulsive. Denouncing arrogance, the psalm describes some people as so awful that they abuse widows/orphans/strangers (if you can imagine it!). (Psalm 94)*

No clear echo in the New Testament.

> 18. *The Babylonian Exile was a punishment for a short list of specific grave evils – including abuse of strangers. The exile was the fourth calamitous response to inhospitality. (Jeremiah)*
>
> 19. *With Jeremiah, another major prophet, Ezekiel, said that the Babylonian Exile was a punishment for inhospitality, among other things.*
>
> 20. *After the Exile, the prophets continued to denounce abuse of strangers in a short list of evils committed by people with "diamond-hard hearts." (Zechariah)*

21. In the final chapter of the Old Testament, the prophet Malachi says that the "refiner's fire" will purge us of evils including inhospitality.

These passages all deal with severe punishments for violating hospitality – as in Sodom, Egypt, and Gibea. This idea does indeed appear in the New Testament. The story of the incarnation, as told is John, can be seen as a story of inhospitality by an entire society. (See #12 above, and chapter 7 below.)

Chapter 2: Diction issues

To find the teaching about strangers including immigrants in the Old Testament, I looked first at all references to strangers, then at stories and images of hospitality. That approach does not work as well with the New Testament. The Old Testament has three words that can be translated into English as "stranger" (actually, seven or more, but three that are particularly significant), and they are very different words. *Ger* is the one that matters, and it is immensely evocative and quite precise. The word is at the center of the best-known story in world literature: the Hebrews were *ger* in Egypt. It's used by Moses to capture the moral lesson from the Exodus; it's found in a long list of laws; and it's used by the prophets in conjunction with widows and orphans. The word's meaning is rich, but emphatically not ambiguous or confusing. The other two words are *nokri*, a more general term meaning "foreign" or perhaps "weird." The third is *zar*, referring specifically to enemies.

Greek has a lot more words that refer to strangers, and even to immigrants; there are eight words to consider, plus different forms of these eight words. None correspond closely to the Hebrew word *ger*. *Xenos* and *paroikos* come closest, and *parepidemos* is pretty close. But other words referring to strangers or being a stranger include *epidemeo*, *allotrios*, and *allogenes*. *Proselutos* needs some discussion; it's not confusing in the New Testament, but it can be a source of confusion in the Septuagint (Greek translation of the Old Testament). *Plesion* is a startlingly complex entry into the mix.

Those are the eight root words, but capturing all the different forms is not a trivial exercise. *Xenos* is worst. *Xenos* means stranger; *xenizo* means to visit and be a guest or stranger, OR to be a host and offer hospitality; *xenia* is a guest room, where guests or strangers stay; *xenodocheo* is to welcome or entertain strangers (or angels); *philoxenia* is the virtue of hospitality. All these words have strong positive connotations almost all the time. Almost always – but *xenos* can refer to a hostile force, the army of your enemies (see Hebrews 13:9).

Music over precision

The word *paroikos* is used four times in the New Testament to refer to strangers. The fourth use is in 1 Peter 2:11. I find it hard to avoid the sense that the author was not choosing his words for precision, but rather for the music in them.

In the Old Testament, which shaped the thinking and writing of New Testament authors, there are many references to strangers. But the warmest are references to "*ger* and *toshab*," two words together, often translated into English as "strangers and sojourners." *Ger* is fairly precise, referring to a person from another land who comes into your land and settles there, who should be treated with respect and with preferential care like a widow or orphan. *Toshab* is similarly positive in connotation, but seems to suggest a bit more transience, like a pilgrim or a sojourner. Elijah had some connection with the town of Tishbe, and is described as *toshab* of Tishbe, or as a "Tishbite sojourner."

So in the New Testament, when two words occur together, referring to strangers, with a clear positive connotation, it seems likely that in Hebrew the speaker referred to a "*ger* and *toshab*." Can we find such a similar common pairing, the first a translation of *ger* and the second a translation of *toshab*? Wouldn't that be nice? I think it would be nice. But it doesn't happen.

Compare two passages, Ephesians 2:19 and 1 Peter 2:11, which seem to echo the repeated references to the pair, *ger* and *toshab*, found all through the Torah. Ephesians: "So then you are no longer strangers [*xenos*] and sojourners [*paroikos*], but you are fellow citizens [*sympolitai*] with the holy ones and members of the household of God." In this passage, *ger* becomes *xenos*, and *toshab* becomes *paroikos*. 1 Peter: "Beloved, I urge you as aliens [*paroikos*] and sojourners [*parepidemos*] to keep away from worldly desires that wage war against the soul." In the second passage, *ger* becomes *paroikos*, and *toshab* becomes *parepidemos*.

Hebrew	ger	toshab
Ephesians	xenos	paroikos
1 Peter	paroikos	parepidemos

I think that the words slide around this way in part because beauty can sometimes outweigh precision. Looking again at the passage from 1 Peter, it seems that the writer wanted a pair of words for strangers or exiles or outsiders or sojourners or some such. He chose *paroikos* and *parepidemos*. Why those two words? I think the answer is musical, not logical. To understand the choice, you don't need to *understand* the Greek, but you do need to *hear* the Greek. The line says, in English: "Beloved, I exhort you, as strangers and pilgrims, to abstain from fleshly things ..." In Greek, the first seven words here are very beautiful. (*Agapetoi parakalo hos paroikous kai parepidemous apechesthai* ...)

The first and seventh words ("beloved" and "abstain") match:

- *agapetoi* and *apechesthai*, four syllables,
- *agap-* matched with *apek-*, and then
- *-etoi* matched with *-esthai*.

The third and fifth words ("as" and "and") are itty bitty bouncy words: *hos* and *kai*.

The second, fourth, and sixth (exhort, stranger, and pilgrim) have delightful alliteration, all beginning with *par-*: *parakalo, paroikous, parepidemous*. How can you resist? You don't have to understand Greek to get the point here. Suppose you are going to *parakalo* some people, and you have several words available to label the people you're going to *parakalo*. You have to say it out loud to get the point. Pick two of the following. I will *parakalo* a ...

- *xenos*, or
- *paroikos*, or
- *parepidemos*.

Assuming that it's not immoral or painful to do this thing, you'd prefer to *parakalo* a *paroikos*, right? And if you're going to add another, you're going to *parakalo* a *paroikos* and a *parepidemos*, right? Right! This is not close, not a serious competition. This is joyful music (not just a dusty old vocabulary lesson). And for music, forget *xenos*. Who wants to *parakalo* a *xenos*?

Bottom line: to figure out what Jesus meant when he talked about welcoming strangers, it was useful to explore the culture he came from, and the precise words of his language, Hebrew. But for the next question, to see whether the clear and forceful teaching from the Old Testament carries over into the New Testament, a Greek concordance is not nearly as useful as a Hebrew concordance was. So I have skipped the diction issues, and decided to dig elsewhere.

Chapter 3: Stranger in his own land

The concern for strangers in the New Testament is more personal than social, unlike the bulk of the teaching on hospitality in the Old Testament, and unlike the teaching of the Church in our own time.

The idea that the stranger knocking at the door might be divine was never lost. But who's responsible for helping the man at the door? The loss of the nation did not change the fundamentals, but did change practical responses; and sorting this out is a challenge.

The teaching in the Old Testament about welcoming strangers included commands directed to individuals, for sure; but the focus of the teaching was on communities and peoples and nations – social welfare and social concerns, city and tribal and national matters. What did *Sodom* do wrong? How should we respond to *Egypt*? Exactly why should we punish the *tribe of Benjamin*? Why will the *kingdom* be crushed and scattered? The actions of individuals mattered: Tobit and Job welcomed strangers into their homes; Boaz took care of Ruth; individual landowners left crops for gleaners. But overall, the teaching about hospitality in the Old Testament was about society more than individuals. That is not the case in the New Testament – or not obviously so.

For one thing, in the time of Jesus, how do you teach the nation? What nation?

When Moses explained the Law to the people or nation of Israel, and when the Prophets called the people or nation to repent, there existed a people or nation that could listen, ponder, and act. But at the time of Jesus, Palestine was under occupation. The seat of government was 1200 miles away, in Rome. There were local leaders, including even a "king" of the Jews; but their power was in the gift of the Romans. The Romans used local leaders and for various administrative tasks; but these men did not have independent power. They were puppets, including the Herodian dynasty who held the throne in Jerusalem; they were wealthy but corrupt. Further, struggling beneath not just one but two levels of civic power, there were religious leaders who – unable to affect serious issues – spent their time wrestling with relatively trivial matters of ritual. So no one at the time of Jesus –

not the state, and not the synagogue – was trying to figure out how the *nation* could or should welcome strangers or immigrants.

How do you deal with foreign conquerors: that was live question. But a national or social policy for immigrants? Not an issue.

The question about who ruled the land came up obliquely in an exchange that Jesus had with Peter. Jesus asked Peter, "From whom do the kings of the earth take tolls or census tax? From their subjects or from foreigners?" Peter responded, "From foreigners." And Jesus remarked, "Then the subjects are exempt," suggesting that – even though they knew they weren't exempt, and Jesus did in fact pull a coin out of nowhere (a fish's mouth) to pay – the people of the land, including Peter and Jesus, *should* be exempt (Mt 17:25-26). But of course they weren't exempt, because they were under occupation.

Later, some Pharisees tried to trap Jesus, pushing him to take a side in a controversy over the census tax – is he with the rebels or the Romans? Jesus points out that the Romans want a coin that has Caesar's image on it; so if they want it back, give it to him. The two conversations were separate, one about the temple tax and the other about the census tax. But taken together, they reveal clearly how Jesus and his disciples felt about their own land. Of course kings collect taxes from foreigners, not subjects; and of course Jesus and disciples are going to pay Caesar's tax. In other words, Jesus and the people to whom he spoke all thought of themselves as strangers, as outsiders, as dispossessed and powerless – in their own land.

In this context, when Jesus addressed the issue of welcoming strangers, he couldn't speak about *social* responsibilities. Instead, he focused on the *personal* responsibilities that remained pertinent regardless of what the government was doing.

The key to continuity: finding the wellspring of sympathy

Despite the challenges and confusion, there is clear continuity between the teaching of Moses and the teaching of Jesus that is worth pondering. This continuity has to do with how the two talked about borders – not national borders between Israel and Egypt, or Palestine and Syria – but the borders or limits of our imaginations. Both faced legalistic questions about whom we should serve — who's a stranger, who's my neighbor — and both responded by challenging our imagination.

In the society that Moses led, there were many different forms of social relations. There were *families*, with close *neighbors*, in *tribes*, which added up to a great *people* or *nation* related by blood, with some *non-Jews* intermingled, aware of many *foreigners* elsewhere in the world, and concerned about some *enemies*. In the society that Jesus taught, there were *families* and there were *neighbors*; but the tribes were scattered, the nation was under occupation, Jews and non-Jews were thoroughly intermingled in many places, and the land was ruled by foreign enemies.

In Moses' society, there were "neighbors," but that was not a particularly important category. It mattered whether someone was part of your family or your tribe, and it mattered whether they were Jewish. But "neighbors"? Of course they existed, but it was not a terribly significant category that required extensive careful thought. It was one relationship amongst many. Non-Jews in their midst: that was a significant issue, requiring thought and care. What should we do about people who live among us, but aren't the same as us? Well, first: who is "us"? That's not too difficult in the Old Testament: it's the story of a nation chosen and tended by God, the Jews. The people who come to live among "us" but choose not to become Jewish are indeed separate from "us" — but, Moses insisted and insisted, they must be treated with respect, as equal in all respects. Identifying the "strangers" in their midst was not complicated, but finding the internal motivation to care about them was a challenge. *Who* was easy; *how* and *why* were complex.

When Moses addressed the issue of care for the strangers in our midst, he urged sympathy. Specifically, he urged there people to recall their own troubles in Egypt, to recall what it meant to live as a stranger in a strange land. If we can recall what we went through, we can understand how to respond to others in the same situation. Use your memory (social memory), he said, to find the wellsprings of sympathy.

In the time of Jesus, "neighbor" was a more significant category. In a broken society, occupied and poverty-stricken, for whom am I responsible? You are responsible for your neighbor, said Jesus. The word "neighbor" appears in the Old Testament, but it's not common; the word for "stranger shows up about ten times as often. So if we are going to focus on loving our "neighbors," the first challenge is, who are they? That's not a trivial question.

When Jesus urged love of neighbors, he was pressed for a definition. He declined to define or limit the term, to draw a line marking who's in and who's out. Instead, he – like Moses – explained how to find the wellsprings of sympathy. He told a story of a man who needs help, and said that the person who gives help is – from the victim's perspective – a neighbor. He said we can find the true line – or the line that matters – between neighbor and non-neighbor by adopting the perspective of the victim.

Who's in? Who's out? Who should get my help? Who should get my love? Moses and Jesus faced the same question, although it was posed in different ways. And they gave the same answer, although they used different details. For both of them, the legal question is secondary, or perhaps completely irrelevant. The real question, both said, is how we learn to love. And they both said, we must get inside the mind and heart and experience of those in need around us.

This is the fundamental continuity from Moses to Jesus. The teaching of Moses about strangers is *identical* to the teaching of Jesus about neighbors: the wellspring of love is not written out in detail in the *law*; rather it is intelligent and imaginative *sympathy*. Find it, and strike the rock! Life-giving water will flow out!

Chapter 4: Good news for all nations

The teaching of Jesus about personal responsibility did not replace the social teaching of Moses. Palestine was occupied, and social response didn't mean much; but Jesus was emphatic that even when the nation or people cannot meet all pertinent responsibilities, individuals should. Jesus did not simply drop the social issue; rather he focused on tougher issue, personal involvement. His teaching about individual responsibility was an addition to Moses' teaching about social responsibility – more of a clarification than a replacement.

There is another potential source of confusion, regarding the mission of Jesus. Were his words pertinent to Jews only, or to all, including strangers?

Jesus' own public ministry was focused on the Jews in a small region. Nonetheless, his intention was clear and explicit: to bring the good news to all nations. To *nations*. And to *all* of them.

His words at the end of Matthew's Gospel are unambiguous: "All power in heaven and on earth has been given to me. Go, therefore, and make disciples of all nations, baptizing them in the name of the Father, and of the Son, and of the Holy Spirit, teaching them to observe all that I have commanded you. And behold, I am with you always, until the end of the age." (Mt 28:18-20)

Did Jesus mean to improve the teaching of Moses, dropping the distracting remarks about the nation's responsibilities, and getting to the real issue – personal responsibility? That doesn't seem to make a lot of sense. It is true that Jesus focused on his own people, his own culture, the Jews. This is fortunate, because it means we can indeed figure out what words like "stranger" mean, because their cultural context can provide clarity. But, emphatically, Jesus did not simply drop the matter of social responsibility. Look at the map of his own work, look at the commission he gave to his disciples, look at … well, look at a list of border-busting issues.

Consider the following.

1. Simeon's Canticle: A light to the Gentiles

Luke's Gospel says the same thing that Matthew's Gospel says: the ministry of Jesus was to Gentiles throughout the world. When Jesus was an infant, and his parents presented him to the Lord at the Temple, a devout man at the temple took Jesus in his arms and prophesied, saying that "my eyes have seen your salvation, which you prepared in sight of all the peoples, a light for revelation to the Gentiles, and glory for your people Israel." This short prophecy, the "Canticle of Simeon," is used in Compline or Night Prayer by priests and monks and religious throughout the world. (Lk 2: 29-32)

2. Galilee: at the border

"When Jesus heard that John had been arrested, he withdrew to Galilee ... that what had been said through Isaiah the prophet might be fulfilled: 'Galilee of the Gentiles, the people who sit in darkness have seen a great light.'" (Mt 4:12-16)

Jesus grew up in Galilee, and began his public ministry there. It was identified as a land of the pagans. That was perhaps an exaggeration; but it was a border territory, where Jews and non-Jews were intermingled. When Jesus spoke of "neighbors," that term included Jews and non-Jews, even before he expanded its meaning.

3. Justice to the Gentiles

"I shall place my spirit upon him, and he will proclaim justice to the Gentiles." Mt 12:18

On another occasion, Jesus healed a man with a withered hand. This was on a Sabbath, and the Pharisees criticized him for it. Matthew says that the incident and reaction were "to fulfill what had been spoken through Isaiah the prophet: "Behold, my servant whom I have chosen, my beloved in whom I delight; I shall place my spirit upon him, and he will proclaim justice to the Gentiles. ... And in his name the Gentiles will hope." Although Jesus said his mission was to the Jews, it was explicit from the outset – indeed, from the time of Isaiah – that this mission affected non-Jews. (Mt 12:17-21)

4. Over the northern border

Jesus went from that place and withdrew to the region of Tyre and Sidon. (Mt 15:21)

Tyre and Sidon are in the land of Canaan, in an area that is now called Lebanon. It was not a part of Israel of Judea, even under King David. In his public ministry, Jesus did not travel far beyond the borders of his nation; but he did cross the line. While he was in Canaan, a local woman asked him to heal her daughter. Jesus replied, "I was sent only to the lost sheep of the house of Israel." She pressed him: "Lord, help me." And he still demurred, in words that seem rude: "It is not right to take the food of the children and throw it to the dogs." The woman tried a third time, and then Jesus praised her faith and healed the daughter. His apparent rudeness is a puzzle. And his statement – in Canaan – that his ministry was the lost sheep of Israel, is also a puzzle. But in the end, he healed the Canaanite girl.

5. Witness to all nations

"And this gospel of the kingdom will be preached throughout the world as a witness to all nations" Mt (24:14).

On his way into Jerusalem at the end of his teaching ministry, Jesus spoke about many topics, including the trails and troubles – and blessings – that would come to his followers. He urges them to take courage and persevere to the end. And he says that the gospel will be preached "throughout the world," and will reach "all nations."

6. Praising an officer of the occupying army

Luke's Gospel records the story of the centurion who asked Jesus for help, and received it. His faith and his gracious manner impressed Jesus, and we use the centurion's words, slightly changed, in every Mass. The centurion was an outsider and a pagan; he may have been concerned that if Jesus entered his house, he would be made unclean. Or he may have been respectful of Jesus' time. For whatever reason, he was keenly aware that he was unworthy to ask the Lord for anything. He asked anyway, but without any arrogance or sense of entitlement. He asked that the Lord heal his servant, but said that Jesus need not actually visit; he could just give the command. His words: "Lord, do not trouble yourself, for I am not worthy to have you enter under my roof ... say the word and let my servant be healed." Jesus praised him: "Not even in Israel have I found such faith." (Lk 7:1-10)

7. The apostles understood their mission to be universal (Acts 2:1-12)

Are not all these people who are speaking Galileans? Then how does each of us hear them in his own native language?

The first miracle of Pentecost was courage: a group of men who had been badly frightened and totally demoralized by the death of Jesus recovered after the resurrection, and in a matter of weeks re-arranged what they had heard all through Jesus' ministry, and then – when the Holy Spirit fell on them like fire – they burst forth, explaining the mysteries of the universe and the fate of mankind. God was in a hurry.

But the second miracle, and the first external "sign" that something new was afoot, was that outsiders understood Peter and the others in their own languages. This was a miracle of hospitality. God had taught a nation about himself through signs and wonders, but also through language – a specific language: Hebrew. Huge parts of what the Lord communicated depend on our ability to situate the revelations within a culture and language. But the first public act of the early Church was to expand the outreach – not only to the Greek-speakers all around them, but also to men and women of every race and tongue.

8. The first challenge to the new church: local or global? (Acts 15:1-31)

The church grew rapidly and joyfully for a period of time, despite persecution – or, some have argued, in part *because of* persecution. But there was a division that festered and grew. And in time, the leaders of the church met in council – in retrospect, Catholics think of it as the first council of 20 so far, the Second Vatican Council being the most recent. This meeting, which

Catholics call the Council of Jerusalem, dealt with a single issue: do you have to become a Jew in order to follow Jesus? Jesus was a Jew, and he followed the Law of Moses; do his followers have to do the same? The question was practical: what do you teach new followers? But it was also a matter of self-definition.

The practical decision was clear: you do not have to keep the ritual and dietary laws of Judaism in order to become a Christian. There were some small compromises, reminders of the Jewish roots of the Church. The larger issue, defining the Church and its relationship to Judaism, was also decided. After Paul, Barnabas, and Peter spoke in favor of an outreach to all the world, non-Jews as well as Jews, James summarized the argument. He said that God did indeed rebuild the fallen hut of David, but it was for a purpose that went beyond the Jews: "so that the rest of humanity may seek out the Lord, even all the Gentiles on whom my name is invoked." The mission is universal – catholic.

9. No longer strangers and sojourners (Eph 2:11-22)

St. Paul, the "missionary to the Gentiles," came back to the issue of unity over and over, urging us to set aside artificial or man-made barriers. God's plan in generous, and we are all called to unity in Christ. Circumcision or non-circumcision should not divide us. Writing to Gentiles, he said: "So then you are no longer strangers and sojourners, but you are fellow citizens with the holy ones and members of the household of God, built upon the foundation of the apostles and prophets, with Christ Jesus himself as the capstone."

10. Paul: break down barriers (Romans 1:14-16)

In his Letter to the Romans, Paul spoke again about artificial barriers that we cannot allow to divide us. "To Greeks and non-Greeks alike, to the wise and the ignorant, I am under obligation; that is why I am eager to preach the gospel also to you in Rome. For I am not ashamed of the gospel. It is the power of God for the salvation of everyone who believes: for Jew first, and then Greek."

It is not possible to read the Gospel honestly and yet divisively. From beginning to end, Jesus reaches out to people beyond any barrier that anyone might want to erect.

11. Hebrews: welcome angels

The essay or letter entitled "Hebrews" echoes the oldest reason in Scripture for welcoming strangers. "Do not neglect hospitality, for through it some have unknowingly entertained angels" (Heb 13:2). The early Church maintained a vivid awareness of Scriptural teaching, and recalled what Abraham learned at Mamre.

It is noteworthy that the passage goes from hospitality to strangers to prisoners. The following line says, "Be mindful of prisoners as if sharing their imprisonment, and of the ill-treated as of yourselves, for you also are in the body." When Jesus described the Last Judgment, his six injunctions included four that we recall easily, and two that we often forget. The familiar four: feed the hungry, give drink to the thirsty, clothe the naked, and visit the sick. Almost everyone forgets that the Lord asked us to welcome the stranger, and many people overlook the injunction to visit the imprisoned.

The Letter of James provides a delightful counterpart to Hebrews. In his acerbic style, James recalls the tone and teaching of the prophets: "Religion that is pure and undefiled before God and the Father is this: to care for orphans and widows in their affliction and to keep oneself unstained by the world" (James 1:27). He mentions the familiar Biblical pair, widows and orphans, without the third in the familiar Biblical trio, strangers. Shortly thereafter, he turns to a controversy that divided the Church deeply 15 centuries later, the artificial division of faith and works. He says, "If a brother or sister has nothing to wear and has no food for the day, and one of you says to them, "Go in peace, keep warm, and eat well," but you do not give them the necessities of the body, what good is it? So also faith of itself, if it does not have works, is dead" (James 2:15-17). Hebrews had two items from Jesus' six injunctions, about strangers and the imprisoned; James has two others, the hungry and the poorly dressed.

It would be convenient to the proof of a specific point about hospitality if James had mentioned strangers explicitly. He doesn't. However, the reason that he and others don't advocate specifically for strangers may be clear in his greeting at the beginning of the letter. He identifies himself as a "slave of God," one of the dispossessed, and addresses the letter to "the twelve tribes in dispersion," also dispossessed. It would be self-serving to speak for strangers; he has joined their ranks, and so have the people whom he addresses. He and his readers *are* strangers.

12. The final tabernacle and tent of the pilgrim

The teaching about welcoming strangers goes through the Gospels, the Letters, and Acts. The final book, Revelation, is complex. It's about where we are aiming to go, about heaven. Revelation is not in code, explaining that the Jewish settlement policy is or isn't going to bring the world to an end. It's about a new home, the place that the Lord prepares for us. It's full of details that require explanation – like any foreign land, but more so. The place is foreign. From here, it looks like a strange land. Put another way: from there, it is clear that we live here and now as strangers in a strange land. The coast of Maine, the mall in Washington, the music of New Orleans, the beaches of Florida, the golden wheat fields of the Midwest, the Grand Canyon, the marriage of mountain and ocean and mankind up and down the Pacific coast – all wonderful, tantalizing, suggestive, perhaps hopeful – but none of it is heaven. Revelation is an effort to fit heaven into our picture of reality, and it's complex. Still, the theme of hospitality does indeed go right straight through to the end. Two points.

First, the vision described in Revelation includes imagery of a battle that leads to ultimate victory. Usually, pictures explain things better than ideas, but Revelation is an exception. It may be easier to duck the imagery for a moment, and return to the conceptual language in Hebrews. Hebrews provides a sweeping vision of faith, including a section that moves from Genesis to the end of time, from the Mamre to the heaven. Faith guided Abel and Enoch and Noah, and then Abraham: "By faith Abraham obeyed when he was called to go out to a place that he was to receive as an inheritance; he went out, not knowing where he was to go. By faith he sojourned in the promised land as in a foreign country, dwelling in tents with Isaac and Jacob, heirs of the same promise" (Heb 11:8-9). This vision goes on to those who saw the Promised Land, but sweeps past them rapidly to get to the real point: "They did not receive what had been promised but saw it and greeted it from afar and acknowledged themselves to be strangers and aliens on earth … But now they desire a better homeland, a heavenly one. Therefore, God is not ashamed to be called their God, for he has prepared a city for them" (Hebrews 11: 13-16). All of us are strangers in a strange land – all, including Abraham and all his descendants – until our pilgrimage ends at strangest of all lands, which is home forever. And Revelation ends up at this home.

It is indeed a strange land, and explaining it requires dragons and jewels and star wars. But the end of the story is in a city, which is recognizable as Jerusalem, although is transformed, made new – like the vision that Peter and James and John had of Jesus in his transfiguration. Peter wanted to provide a tent for the Lord, and was hushed up; here it is at last. In this bewildering new world, where the city is a Bride loved by the Lamb, where almost everything is strange and even the familiar is made new, there is a detail of familiarity: the host who provides water for the thirsty is the one who sits on the throne. If we welcomed strangers on earth, we will recognize the Stranger in heaven, with joy for sure, but perhaps with some surprise and relief as well. God visited Abraham in his tent. And God cared for his people as they carried the Ark of the Covenant on their long pilgrimage – the Ark, the tabernacle, the Tent. And God came to dwell among us – in John's words, "pitching his tent among us." In John's vision, the voice from the throne declares, "Behold, God's dwelling is with mankind. He will dwell with them and they will be his people and God himself will always be with them." This is Emmanuel, the Lord who offers us hospitality forever.

Transition point: From argument to application

Have I reached the point where I can stop arguing, and just show you something wonderful? I have written about 30,000 words to prove a point – that hospitality to strangers is all over the Old Testament, and that this forceful teaching continues into the New Testament. Can I change my approach? Can I assume that the teaching is valid, and point out things that show up in the bright light of that teaching? I hope so.

From this point forward, I would like to shift my approach a bit. In 21 Stranger Claims in the Old Testament, *I tried to prove convincingly that Scriptural teaching about welcoming strangers is abundant and clear and forceful. In the first chapters of this volume, I tried to show convincingly that the abundant teaching on the Old Testament didn't just evaporate into thin air in the New Testament, leaving only a few traces. Rather, it continued as forcefully as in the Old Testament, but from a different angle: hospitality among nation-builders is different from hospitality in an occupied nation, but the obligation is personal and eternal, not only social. I have tried not to be blindingly grindingly repetitive, just deliberately convincingly repetitive. But after saying the same thing 40 times – welcome strangers and meet the Father joyfully or don't and make your own eternal accommodations with less joy – I'd like to assume the point is made, and use it. Hospitality is a ray of light, like chastity or martyrdom, shining blindingly straight from the glowing heart of the Lord. The light is a thing of beauty. It's there, and once you see it, you can't un-see it, and it's all over creation and revelation. So now – what do we see in that light?*

Up to now, I have tried to be scrupulous about not forcing the text, not cherry-picking to find scattered lines to make a pre-conceived point. For example, I am convinced that the names of Moses two sons are tremendously significant, two sides of a single revelation. And I am convinced that this lesson is in the text, objectively, demonstrably. But I am not at all convinced – to pick a single example – that the demonic temptations of Jesus after his time in the desert are a caricature of the hospitality in Mamre. I find it interesting and enlightening to make the comparison, noting that the exchange with the devil includes bread, foot care, and bowing. But is that comparison really in the text, or is it just my preoccupation that I am imposing on the text? Truthfully, I don't really know. I think it's there in the text, objectively. But I am not sure – and from this point forward, I don't really care. Even if the passage about the devil's offers is not a caricature of hospitality, it's still worthwhile to look at it from the perspective of hospitality. So from this point forward, I will not be quite as scrupulous about proof. Instead, I intend to use the light.

Chapter 5: Angels and strangers (Matthew)

There are three infancy narratives in the four Gospels, in Matthew and Luke and John. (Mark does not have an infancy narrative.) All three infancy narratives have fascinating references to the status of strangers.

Matthew's Gospel begins with the genealogy of Jesus, a list of who begat whom for generations. The list is in three pieces, recalling the history of Israel in three pieces: from Abraham to David, from David to the Babylonian Exile, and from the Babylonian Exile to Joseph. Matthew uses the genealogy to place Jesus systematically within a clear historical context. It is interesting that each of the transition points in the genealogy includes some insight into hospitality.

The genealogy begins with the patriarch of the Jewish people, Abraham. The story of Abraham fills a quarter of the Book of Genesis, the beginning of the Bible; of those 12 chapters, two are about hospitality. Abraham set the pattern of Jewish hospitality at Mamre, welcoming three strangers who turned out to be God and two angels.

The second great figure in the genealogy is David. David was a complex figure: shepherd, lion-killer, warrior, musician, adulterer and murderer who repented, and a great king. There is a strange detail included carefully in his biography: his great-grandmother was Ruth the Moabite. She was a remarkable woman: eloquent, decisive, determined, feminine, faithful. It's plausible that her story is preserved in Scripture because she was the source of many of David's personal traits. But also: she was a stranger, an immigrant from Moab. David, the greatest king in Israel's history, was proud of his foreign ancestry.

The third major point in the genealogy is not a person but an event, the Babylonian Exile. Jeremiah and Ezekiel warned the people of the land that they would be punished severely unless they turned away from several grave evils, including idolatry and injustice to the poor – and mistreating strangers. Before and during and after the exile, prophets tied to the national trauma to a national evil: inhospitality.

So the genealogy has three sections. The first section starts with Abraham, who was the host to angels, and ends with David, whose great-grandmother was Ruth the Moabite stranger. The second section is from David to the Babylonian Exile, punishment for inhospitality. The third section is from the Babylonian Exile to Joseph, who took his family into acute stranger-dom: exile in Egypt.

The story of Joseph and the Holy Family – the rest of chapter 1 after the genealogy, and then chapter 2 – includes ten references to hospitality.

1. Take Mary into your home

When Joseph learns that Mary is pregnant, without his help, he is understandably concerned. But an angel appears to him in a dream, and tells him to accept Mary's incredible story. The angel's word to Joseph is couched in terms of hospitality: take her into your home. When Joseph chooses to be obedient and cooperative, the description of what he does is again couched in terms of hospitality: he does take her into his home. This is one of the many times in Scripture when the relationship between a host and guest is described in ways that resemble the unity of marriage.

2. Joseph protected Mary and her child from becoming widow and orphan, or worse

If Joseph had rejected Mary's story, she and Jesus would have been set aside, unprotected. She would have been faced with the difficulties of a woman with a child, without the help and support of the social standing of a man, in a patriarchal society. Obviously, she would not have been a widow, nor would Jesus have been an orphan; but she would have had the practical problems of a widow, without the protections that Moses put in place. Pro-life activists today see her as a sympathetic figure, someone who understands the hazards of being an unwed mother. She was at risk of being like a widow, with an orphan, alienated.

3. The baby's names: hospitality and salvation

The angel who speaks to Joseph tells him that the child will be called "Emmanuel," which means "God is with us." The name sounds angelic – like Rapha-el and Gabri-el and Micha-el. The name recalls the experience of Abraham, who welcomed strangers into his home, and found himself in the presence of God. But when the baby was born, he was not given the angelic name, at least not for daily use; he was instead named Jesus, which means "savior." This pair of names resembles those that Moses gave his two sons, Gershom and Eliezer. "Gershom" incorporates the evocative Hebrew word *ger*, and refers to hospitality; "Eliezer" refers to God – El – as a rescuer. Similarly, Joseph's newborn baby is called "Emmanuel," referring to hospitality (among other things), and "Jesus," referring to salvation.

4. Strangers: first to proclaim the good news

Mary and Joseph understood where the baby was from, and knew something cosmic was afoot; but in Matthew's account we don't hear anything else about anyone else who knew anything much – until a group of foreigners showed up. The magi from the east didn't understand Jewish politics, but something in the stars had somehow alerted them to the birth of a new king of the Jews. They did not have (or, anyway, didn't display) a clear understanding of who Jesus was or what he would do; but they knew something was happening. And they were the first to announce it publicly. In a sense, these strangers can be called the *first disciples* of Jesus, and the *first evangelists*, although their understanding was incomplete.

5. The magi entered as guests

When the magi found Jesus, they entered the house. The most common Greek words for "stranger" are *xenos* and *paroikos*; *paroikos* means someone who is near but not in (*para-*) the house (*oikos*). Entering a house is a significant event. The magi didn't just step through a rough entrance; when they entered the physical structure, they also entered into a complex relationship, a host/guest relationship, with Joseph and his family.

6. Flight to Egypt: the Holy Family as prototype of refugees

When Joseph fled with Mary and Jesus into Egypt, they became the prototype of refugees. Since then, the Church has portrayed or explained refugees using the image of the Holy Family trekking south, often with Mary and her baby on a donkey led by Joseph. The Catholic Church in our day, asking us to welcome immigrants and refugees, still points to this event, this image. Joseph was a carpenter, a laborer, fleeing into a land where he didn't have a job and didn't know the language. His wife had a newborn baby who didn't have any of his genes, and might not have looked a lot like Joseph. And the cops were after them for some reason.

7. Joseph the stranger

When Joseph took Mary into his home, he protected her and her child from something like widow-orphan status, but even more alienated. In the flight to Egypt, to protect them again, Joseph left behind his status as native-born, and took on the status of stranger.

8. Strangers in a strange land

In summing up the moral lessons of the Exodus, Moses said, "Welcome strangers, because – remember! – you too were once a stranger in a strange land." Joseph and Mary did not just *recall* the lesson from the far-distant past; they lived it out. They *became* strangers in a strange land – like Moses, whose steps they re-traced.

9. Egypt, a safe refuge

When the Holy Family found a safe refuge in Egypt, that was good for them – but it was also good for Egypt. It is plausible to argue that the first healing worked by Jesus was to repair a nation, to give Egypt a second chance. Centuries before, when Jacob – re-named Israel – went down to Egypt with his sons, and found the long-lost and rejected son there ready to save them, Egypt took them in for a while, and then turned against them and enslaved them. At the time of Moses, Egypt sinned grievously against the Hebrews – and against hospitality, and against the God who cherished the Hebrews and demanded hospitality. Now, this harshly judged and long-maligned nation gets another chance to offer hospitality. And this time, they succeed.

10. Not welcome in Israel

When Joseph brought his family back from Egypt, they were still not completely welcome in their own land. So they went to a border region, Galilee, where there were many other Jews, but also many non-Jews. They settled down in a town where differences did not divide.

The list of links between the infancy narrative and the concept of hospitality do not prove that hospitality matters. Rather, accepting the reality of hospitality as a key element of revelation, as a ray of divine light, we can see new aspects of this familiar story.

Chapter 6: Mary's story of the birth (Luke)

The birth narrative in the Gospel of Luke, like that in Matthew, is loaded with insights into hospitality.

1. Zechariah was inhospitable in some way

"Do not be afraid, Zechariah ... but now you will be speechless and unable to talk."

Oops. Luke's Gospel begins with remarks about the reason for writing the account, then sets the scene a little, then plunges in – not with a long list of begats like Matthew, but with two conceptions and two births. The first incident in the narrative is the experience of Zechariah, father of John the Baptist, in the temple. The incident recalls Mamre is several ways. Zechariah and his wife Elizabeth are old and childless, like Abraham and Sarah. Zechariah is offering a sacrifice. A sacrifice is definitely not the same thing as a dinner; but sacrifices are related to feasts, and the two often occur together. A sacrifice, like the feast at Mamre, is an encounter between God and man. So when Luke's Gospel begins, an angel appears, and this recalls Mamre, although the angel is a little less gentle than the strangers at Mamre.

Zechariah offends the angel in some way. The offense is not quite in the open; his words are very similar to Mary's words in a similar situation shortly after this, and yet her words were completely acceptable and his were not. He said, "How do I know?" and she said, "How can that happen?" It might be entertaining to argue about the difference between knowledge and being, between epistemology and ontology; but I think that most people would consider the responses to be pretty similar on the surface. It seems that in our dealings with God (or angels), what matters is not so much what we say or do as the spirit we bring to our response. And it seems clear – not from the words but from the response – that the angel was offended by Zechariah's doubt, which resembled Mary's incomprehension only superficially. That is, if an angel approaches you, listen and learn and cooperate. The heart of hospitality is not the act of bowing, which can be faked; it's respect.

2. Mary's response: service, proper hospitality

The angel Gabriel was sent from God to a town of Galilee ... "Hail, favored one! The Lord is with you." But she was greatly troubled at what was said and pondered what sort of greeting this might be.

When the angel visited Mary, she was perplexed and had questions. But her underlying stance, her attitude, becomes clear before the encounter is over: "Behold, I am the handmaid of the Lord. May it be done to me according to your word." She knows who she is, and when she explains herself to the angel, it sounds exactly right. Her identity is built on the Lord: talk about building on solid ground. She knows what she wants, and when she voices it, you know with calm certainty that her prayer will be heard. Her prayer is indistinguishable from God's command. Her words are brief and simple, but rich enough to ponder forever. One detail: she listens respectfully, and her service is hospitable.

3. Visitation: response to revelation is hospitality.

"Mary set out and traveled to the hill country in haste to a town of Judah, where she entered the house of Zechariah and greeted Elizabeth."

Why did Mary go see Elizabeth? For advice? To help the older woman? To share her joy? To think? All of the above and a lot more? Why does anyone ever visit anyone else?

Hospitality is a two-way street: it's hospitable to receive visitors, and it's hospitable to visit. In his description of the Last Judgment, Jesus lists six things we must do, including welcoming strangers and visiting the sick and imprisoned. Hospitality is portable: if they can't visit you, you visit them. Sometimes you know who's host and who's guest, but sometimes you don't; sometimes the two are intertwined, inextricable. In Jesus' list of six, the word (in Greek) for welcoming strangers is *synago*, as in *synagogue*. It's not passive, sitting at home waiting for a knock; it's proactive. Hens "synagogue" their chicks; farmers "synagogue" their crops; fishermen "synagogue" fish. The word means to go get them, sweep them up, bring them in! So Mary's visit is on Elizabeth's property, but it is still "hospitable." Elizabeth is pleased to see her, and welcomes her in hospitably. *Both* are hospitable.

Why visit? This question is, lamentably, identifiable as a First World question, in the 20th-21st century. Hospitality is a form of love; it brims over unless you bottle it up tight.

4. Who is worthy to receive such a guest?

Elizabeth cried out, "And how does this happen to me, that the mother of my Lord should come to me?"

There's a little bit of a tangle there, when you try to sort out who's more important than whom. Elizabeth is the elder. But in some mysterious or miraculous way she knew that Mary was carrying a baby, and also knew something about this baby. So she was respectful of the baby and the baby's mother, and considered herself to be subordinate. How long did that silliness last? Was it like kids playing in a pool: who can touch the bottom and stay there longest? Both mothers were living in the presence of beings who inspire awe. But I think they got around to chattering and laughing promptly. Mary probably washed off her feet, but I can't see Mary letting Elizabeth get the water. We don't know; whatever we say about it is almost 100% conjecture. Probably they swapped wild stories. Probably they swapped pregnancy stories. Probably they sang. And I bet they baked. What isn't conjecture is joy; that's recorded, explicitly.

Who is worthy to receive such a guest? The question is not answered; rather, it's submerged in joy.

5. John the Baptist leaps: hospitality is a joy

"The infant in my womb leaped for joy."

It wasn't just the two women who cried out and sang; Elizabeth said that her baby went a little crazy too. Her description of what she experienced might be controversial today: what is the emotional range of a fetus? Can a baby feel pain or joy at that age and stage? She thought so. It was her impression that the joy of the visit was not just between the two adults, but was also shared by the babies – or at least one of them. The experience of hospitality was an experience of joy, overflowing joy.

6. Magnificat: a host to the poor

The hungry he has filled with good things.

Luke says that during the visit in the hills, Mary produced a canticle of stunning beauty. Some scholars, faced with the poem, hunt around for a scrivener with a scroll, and suggest that the poem was written decades later and then placed in her mouth for effect. That strikes me as an answer in search of a question. Why can't an intelligent young woman – raised on the poetry in the psalms, accustomed to an oral tradition, who has recently been spending time with at least one angel and then the Most High, given hours walking alone through the hills – produce a poem on her own, and remember it, and sing it 50 years later?

Mary's poem is a love song. She has met someone whom she loves, who touches and fills the deepest part of her heart. He has transformed her, and his greatness fills her. She loves his name, and loves everything he does. And one of the things that he does that she loves is to provide hospitality to the poor.

7. Zechariah's song: God has visited us.

Blessed be the Lord, the God of Israel, for he has visited and brought redemption to his people.

When John is born, Zechariah recovered his voice, and prophesied. His whole canticle is beautiful, and there is abundant reason for the Church to chant or sing it every morning. But a detail of it is noteworthy: it begins and ends talking about God visiting us. The words are often obscured a little: "He has come to his people and set them free" and "the dawn from on high shall break upon us." The Greek word is *episkeptomai*, to visit, to go see. It's the word used in the description of the Last Judgment, for visiting the sick and imprisoned (Mt: 25:36 and Mt: 25:43). It's the word used in Hebrews, quoting a Psalm: "What is man that you are mindful of him, or the son of man that you care for [visit] him?" (Heb 2:6). It's used in James: "Religion that is pure and undefiled before God and the Father is this: to care for [visit] orphans and widows in their affliction" (James 1:27).

It's worth slowing down a little to get this line right. Zechariah cries out: bless God for two things he has done. First, he has visited us, has come to live with us. Second, he has saved us. Zechariah speaks of redemption as an accomplished fact, although the death and resurrection of Jesus are still decades in the future, because he knows that if the Lord is among us, the completion of his work is imminent. The incarnation includes all that follows, with all its myriads of details and all its complexity. It's almost unimaginable how much Zechariah packed into that prophetic statement: he has set us free. There is so much packed in that we can (and almost always do?) overlook that Zechariah said two things. The second is salvation; but the first is, God made us the objects of his proactive hospitality. Recall: Moses took two lessons from the Exodus: we should care for strangers, and we should thank God for saving us. The same here: Zechariah speaks of hospitality and salvation. *Episkeptomai*: to visit, to check on, to care for.

At the end of the canticle, Zechariah repeats it, and we generally overlook it again. God (the dawn from on high), in his tender compassion, will (1) visit us – breaking into our world, breaking upon us pro-actively and forcefully – and (2) bring us to a new world of light and peace. Zechariah's prophecy is about incarnation and salvation *both*, Christmas and Easter *both*. Let's not skip Christmas!

The idea of God visiting us may get lost in the image of the dawn breaking in. It's hard to make both the sunrise and the proactive visit clear in a word or two. But if we focus for a moment on the sunrise, it may get clearer. The image shows up in the last book of the Old Testament, in Malachi. The prophet describes the "messenger of the covenant," who will prepare the way before the Lord. He will be like a refiner's fire, and he will purify a sinful people, refining them like gold or silver. He will purify the people from their sins, including six specifically: sorcery, adultery, perjury, cheating laborers, oppressing widows and orphans, and turning aside strangers (Mal 3:5). (Note well! Hospitality to strangers is not the only thing on his mind, but it is one item in a short list, just six items.) But for those who survive the purification, "the sun of justice will arise with healing in its wings" (Mal 3:20). The "sun of justice": this is the same dawn that Zechariah speaks about, the dawn that will break upon us, the light that will visit us and care for us: *episkeptomai*.

8. No room at the inn

There was no room for them in the inn.

Christmas pageants for hundreds of years have made much of this detail, so it can be a shock to notice that it's actually just a single line in the text. For some significant truths, you have to slow down and read carefully to catch it! When Jesus came among us, the son of the Creator, in an act of unbelievable proactive hospitality, we made room for him – which was good. But just barely – which is a problem.

9. The shepherds' visit was a delight.

They went in haste and found Mary and Joseph, and the infant lying in the manger.

There are many thing that can be said (have been said) about the visit of shepherds to the Good Shepherd. But one detail: the visit was satisfactory on both sides. After the shepherds left, Mary kept the words they had spoken, the story they told, the vision of angels they had seen – "reflecting on them in her heart" (Lk 2:19). And the shepherds, for their part, returned to work "glorifying and praising God for all they had heard and seen" (Lk 2:20). They didn't exchange any gifts other than words, but it was a wonderful visit.

10. The expanding circle of revelation

It is worth reviewing who heard about the birth of Jesus, and understood that it was a wonderful event even if they didn't grasp the full import. Zechariah at the temple heard about his own son, but not about Jesus. Mary was the first to hear about what was happening – which was obviously appropriate, since it happened inside her womb. In Luke's account, Elizabeth is next. Zechariah was next, understanding at least that his son John was the one who was to go before the Lord. Joseph is in the story, but Luke's account does not explain when or how he learned what was happening. And next are the shepherds. They were not Gentiles or foreigners, but they were strangers to Mary. Next were people in the temple. So the news of this world-changing birth was known to two families – Jesus' and John's families – and then, next, to strangers. The channels of communication through the temple came *after* angels told some strangers about the birth.

11. Simeon: a light to the strangers

"My eyes have seen … a light for revelation to the Gentiles."

When the newborn Jesus was presented at the temple, Simeon held the child and thanked God for what he saw. He saw history changing – for all Israel, but also for the world. He didn't understand all that was to come, but he did know that this child would transform life for all – for his nation, but also for foreigners, strangers – Gentiles.

12. Who received whom?

The first two chapters of Luke's Gospel are jam-packed with instances of hospitality. An angel visits Zechariah, and it works out – but with a glitch. An angel visits Mary, whose response re-defines the model of hospitality, getting to the heart of what Abraham had done. Mary receives the Most High, but we don't hear a single word about it, and don't know much about it until we get to Pentecost, probably; and even then it's not clear. Mary visits Elizabeth, in proactive hospitality. The fetal John welcomed the embryonic Jesus, in some fashion. An innkeeper provided humble shelter for the Lord of the Universe. Mary greeted her newborn son, wrapping him up and laying him to rest. The shepherds have a wonder-filled visit with Mary. And at the temple, Simeon and Anna greeted and welcomed Jesus. It's like reading Jane Austen: studies in hospitality – not on every page, but in every chapter!

Chapter 7: Glory, grace and truth (John)

John's account of the arrival of Jesus in our world is not a down-to-earth no-room-at-the-inn story. It's cosmic, starting with a quick re-write of Genesis. "In the beginning, when God created the heavens and the earth" becomes "In the beginning was the Word, and the Word was with God, and the Word was God." Genesis goes on, explaining that on the first day, "God said: Let there be light, and there was light." John explains that a little: the Word brought life, "and this life was the light of the human race; the light shines in the darkness, and the darkness has not overcome it." This is the "cosmic Christ." John does not emphasize or even mention the swaddling clothes.

The background and the frame for the story as John tells it is unlike the frame the other Evangelists chose. John is speaking of the same person, but from a different perspective. That makes the beginning of the action, the first piece of a narrative, even more dramatic. John, like Matthew and Luke, explains that when Jesus arrived, he was treated as a stranger – and in fact, maltreated in a familiar pattern of abuse of strangers. "He was in the world, and the world came to be through him, but the world did not know him."

All mankind was alienated from the world, and from God, beginning when Adam and Eve were banished from the Garden of Eden. But Abraham – prodded by God – had worked out a way to deal with that alienation, at least in part. When strangers showed up at Abraham's tent, Abraham treated them with great respect, as if they were celestial beings. So when it turned out that he was in fact dealing with God and angels, it was not a shock and an embarrassment. It was okay that he hadn't recognized who his visitors were; he had treated them appropriately.

When Jesus came, "the world did not know him." That's sad, but it's okay – as long as people follow Abraham's example. But as John's story unfolds, people did not recognize him – and then they treated this "stranger" badly. In fact, they (we) eventually crucified him.

In fact, John records tersely the worst instance of inhospitality in the history of the universe. The Word of God, through whom the world was made, came into the world, and "the world did not know him." In fact, the Gospel specifies, he came to his own people, and "his own people did not accept him." The first is sad; the second is a disaster.

The word translated here as "accept," is *paralambano*, another extraordinarily potent word in Greek, like the word *synago* for "welcome." *Paralambano*: that's what Joseph did when he took (*paralambano*) Mary into his home as his wife, despite her puzzling pregnancy. It's what Joseph did when he picked up (*paralambano*) Jesus and fled to Egypt with Mary. It's what the devil did when he took (*paralambano*) Jesus up on a high place to tempt him. It's what Jesus did when he took (*paralambano*) the 12 apostles aside on their way into Jerusalem. It's what Jesus did when he took (*paralambano*) Peter and James and John to the Garden of Gethsemane Holy Thursday night.

Paralambano is not a weak verb like "get" or "go". It's a fat five-syllable word, which is a hint; it's another proactive go-get-them-and-twist-their-arms kind of verb, with some force: not just "c'm 'ere," more like "come-ity-come-bomb."

Jesus came into the world, and the world didn't accept him. "Accept": what does that mean? The world didn't say "yep"? What was the world supposed to do? The world was supposed to lay hold of him and make him our own, take his arm and make sure we are walking together, unite our mind and his mind, make sure our path is his path, open wide our door and bow and urge him to come in and stay awhile while we give him some bread and prepare him a feast.

"His own people did not accept him." That sounds as if they (we) didn't "accept" his claim that he was the Messiah, and indeed the Son of God. The world didn't "accept" that either; but emphatically, that's not what the text says here. This is not about whether we accepted an idea; it's about whether we reached out proactively to welcome this person, like Joseph taking Mary (and the fetal savior) into our homes.

People didn't recognize Jesus: that's not perfect, but it's not a surprise. But when this person arrived and was mis-identified as a stranger, he was then subjected to ferocious xenophobia, in shocking violation of Moses' clear and repeated and urgent demand: welcome strangers! This is not a problem in the mind; it's a problem in the heart! The failure to *paralambano* was not a misunderstanding; it was a grave sin! It was not bad doctrine; it was bad practice, mal-practice, mortal omission!

In our time, we have a couple of colossal barriers to understanding the problem of our inhospitality to the Lord when he arrived. For one thing, in our time, hospitality is often understood as a decoration, a matter of good manners, of decorum. To us, it's relatively trivial. Second, despite more than a century of teaching expanding the "social gospel," despite the Second Vatican Council's insistence that we re-position ourselves in order to be the Church in the modern world, despite the clear teaching from St. Pope John Paul II about social concerns and social sin, we are still struggling to understand this whole non-individual thing. It's common for good people to turn to the Church for advice about the liturgy and sex, and then refuse to listen to what the Church says about justice. So, to put the world's inhospitality to the Lord in context, we should back up and review four instances of this social sin of inhospitality in the Old Testament: Sodom, Egypt, Gibea, and Babylon.

The cities of the plain, especially Sodom and Gomorrah, offended God. Angels visited to investigate, and were met with inhospitality and attempted homosexual gang rape. Isaiah, recalling the sins of Sodom in order to call the people of Judah to repentance, cries out to princes of Sodom: "Make justice your aim!" He complains bitterly about those who indulge in luxury in the midst of need. Jeremiah also decries growing evil in the land and recalls Sodom to make his point. The people have become like Sodom, he says; that is, they have fallen into idolatry, adultery, and injustice, siding with the strong and wicked against the poor. Ezekiel also: "Now look at the guilt of your sister Sodom!" What is this guilt? Sodom and her daughters were proud, sated with food, complacent in prosperity; they did not give any help to the poor and needy. The sin of Sodom, as the angels see and the prophets explain, is luxury, injustice, inhospitality – so extreme that they want to use strangers as toys for their pleasure. The corporate punishment for this social evil was fire and brimstone obliterating the cities.

The nation of Egypt abused the Hebrew people. They helped them for a time when Jacob and his family moved to Egypt as economic refugees fleeing from famine. But over time, the Egyptians turned against the foreigners, and enslaved them. In fact, the powerful and arrogant nation launched a campaign of deliberate genocide against the Hebrews. Moses, recalling the evil that led up to the Exodus, does not refer to the treachery or the genocide. Instead, he repeats, over and over, two other aspects of the experience. First, we were enslaved until God set us free – so be grateful. And second, we were strangers in a strange land who were abused – so we should never do that to strangers in our midst. Moses focused on two points: God's salvation and the demands of hospitality. And the corporate punishment for this social evil was ten plagues and the destruction of the army at the Red Sea.

The town of Gibea assaulted a stranger and his concubine who were passing through. Their sins included: inhospitality, attempted homosexual gang rape, and murder. But when the army of Israel gathered to avenge the wrongs and asked for a summary of why they were fighting, the victim's summation referred to the inhospitality and murder, without mentioning the attempted rape. The corporate punishment for this social evil was the same as at Sodom: the inhabitants were killed and the city was burned.

Centuries after the days of glory under King David, God's people drifted into a renewed pattern of careless sin, including idolatry, adultery, injustice, and inhospitality. Jeremiah and Ezekiel invoke the horrible example of Sodom, and warned the nation to repent. If they did break away from their evil habits, they would be smashed. They did not repent, and they were invaded. The corporate punishment for their social evils included the destruction of the city and the exile to Babylon.

Each of these grave evils was a social evil. Each time, there several different overlapping crimes – murder, rape, idolatry, thoughtless luxury amidst poverty, injustice to the poor, inhospitality to strangers. Sins against hospitality did not stand alone as the primary crime, in any case; but inhospitality was on the short list of crimes, in all cases.

So when John says that Jesus was not received hospitably, this is not a sideshow. No matter how venial that sin sounds to the modern ear, John was making a most serious charge. The grave evil that began with a sin of omission – a failure to welcome Jesus, whether or not it was clear who he was – culminated in murder, and in fact regicide, and in fact deicide. What's a just punishment for that? Damnation for everyone sounds like a good start. Maybe destroying the universe. But in fact, the punishment included the death of the king – the Lamb, the King, the Priest, the Victim. Jesus took the whole penalty on himself. The King was punished for the world's crime of inhospitality to the King (among other evils).

	Inhospitality: crime and punishment			
	crime	culprit	Victim	Punishment
Sodom	Luxury, inhospitality, homosexual gang rape	People of Sodom	visitors	Fire and brimstone
Exodus	Genocide, slavery inhospitality	Egyptian ruler and army	Hebrew immigrants	10 plagues, army drowned
Gibea	Inhospitality, rape, attempted homosexual gang rape, murder	People of Gibea	visitors	War, cities razed
Babylon	Injustice, idolatry, inhospitality	People of Israel	The poor and strangers	Exile
Herod (and all humanity)	Idolatry, ingratitude, inhospitality	world	God	Crucify the king

He pitched his tent among us

The penalties for inhospitality are immense, but John continues sketching the blessings for those who were hospitable: "To those who did accept him, he gave the power to become children of God." And what does that look like? John, who doesn't rely much on visual or tangible detail, explains the upside of hospitality: "Glory … glory … grace and truth … grace … grace … grace and truth."

"The Word became flesh," John says, "and made his dwelling among us." John starts his account by identifying Jesus as the Word of God, the Word that was present at the beginning. Then, continuing to tell the story with his eye on Genesis, John says that this same Word has come to dwell among us. That is, the curse of

Adam – the exile from the Garden of Eden – is not ended, but it's transformed. Outside the Garden, we find God among us. Further, with his eye still on Genesis, John uses a word for "dwell" that evokes the memory of Abraham, the wandering Aramean. The word that John uses – *eskeinosen*, from *skeinei*, tent – means he "pitched his tent." God shows up among us, as he did when he visited Abraham in *his* tent at Mamre; but this time, God has come to stay.

The language that John uses is abstract rather than concrete, but there are extraordinarily rich images lurking just behind his words. "Glory" is *doxa* in Greek, *kavod* in Hebrew. In the Exodus, God appeared to Moses and the people as a cloud by day and a fire by night: *kavod*. As the long trek through the wilderness continued, they built a tabernacle for the tablets with the Law of Moses, and the *kavod* of the Lord dwelt among the people, in the tabernacle. The glory of the Lord inspired awe, even fear: when Moses spent time alone with the Lord, some of the Lord's *kavod* still shone from his face, and he wore a veil to avoid terrifying people. When Jesus, the Word of God, came to dwell among us, John says, those who accepted him as a guest saw this glory.

Grace: what's that? It's a gift, and when we receive such gifts, we should be grateful. But what is it? You can't package it; it's a way of moving, a way of living, a way of being. The Greeks said that a good life was based on beauty and truth and goodness; grace combines two these in an unearned gift, beauty and goodness.

Truth: one detail of the Word who has come to live among us is that Truth is a gift to us from this Word. Mahatma Gandhi spoke of Truth as God, as the highest good. He urged people not only to speak in such a way that our words are always true but also to live in such a way that our lives correspond to Truth. John puts it differently. Glory and grace and truth come from this Word. This Word is the source of things as immense and important as glory and grace and truth.

Eucharist: the root of this complex word is *charis*, grace. Eucharist means thanksgiving: it is a graceful (grace-filled) response to gifts from God. At the Eucharist, where is the grace? Who initiates grace? Who gives thanks? God gives everything, and we accept the gifts and give thanks to him. God initiates everything. And yet, we are not passive receivers, watching what he does and applauding. He pours grace *on* us, but also *through* us. When David wanted to build a temple for the Lord, the Lord balked; it doesn't work that way, or it's a little complicated. God is the giver of all good things, the source of the universe, and he doesn't need our gifts. But he does want our love, does delight in us and in our free gift of love. He is the host of the universe, and we are his guests; but he is pleased to accept our hospitality, our relatively crude hospitality. The greatest gift he gives us is love, to us and through us. The love that he pours out on us pours through us, coming out of us in two ways: in thanks to God and service to others.

John's language is packed, infinitely dense, reaching out for layer after layer of meaning, touching mystery after mystery: creation, the Exodus, Abraham's tent at Mamre, the Eucharist … One aspect of this shockingly complex account, one ray of light and warmth from the heart of God, is hospitality. God came to dwell among us, Lord and brother and stranger, host and guest.

John's account of the Word who came among his own and was neither recognized nor embraced presents a binary choice, life or death. The account is in a series, coming after Sodom and Egypt and Gibea and Babylon: rejecting the stranger is extraordinarily hazardous. But the blessings that come to those who accept the Lord are rich far beyond our imagination – glory and grace and truth. This choice is presented to us in tiny kernels – not only in the baby at Christmas, but also in every unborn child, every beggar, every immigrant.

Chapter 8: Temptation in the desert

To initiate his public ministry, Jesus went out into the desert to pray. At the end of this, the devil met him, and offered some suggestions about his work. There were three temptations, which are often described as the world, the flesh, and the devil – first, bread, or the flesh; then power, or the world; and finally, idolatry, or the devil. But another plausible interpretation of the temptation story, an additional layer of meaning, sees the devil's offerings as a parody of hospitality.

Jesus was ending his fast, and is would be appropriate to offer bread. The devil offers bread, but with all sorts of added meaning. It is appropriate to add meaning to the bread, but not the meaning the devil offers. Jesus and all the descendants of Abraham – and nearly all humanity – see bread as a sign of unity. The devil offers food from stones as a proof of magic power. Jesus did indeed use signs and wonders to identify and explain himself, but never simply to impress. Multiplying food simply to impress is crude. Further, it's a mockery of the Eucharist.

The devil does not offer to break bread with Jesus. He doesn't offer to share. Why not? Perhaps because the devil is too exalted to eat bread with a mortal, but too degraded to break bread with God.

Throughout the exchange, the devil has his attention fixed on the future – not eternity, but the future. The devil offers to impress people – soon, when you do these things. By contrast, Jesus has his eye on eternity, which shows up in the present moment, the NOW. Jesus was aware: "The kingdom of God IS breaking into the life of mankind – NOW!"

Hospitality following Abraham's pattern would likely include providing water to wash the guest's feet. The devil does not offer that, but does suggest that Jesus line up some servants to care for his feet – specifically, angels to keep him from dashing his foot against a stone. This is overkill: let's take care of the dust, not broken bones. And also, it's off center: a host seeks to make a guest welcome here, now – not just to prepare the guest to elsewhere, later. A time of rest is an appropriate gift, and it does include a preparation for going on. But mostly it's about NOW: relax here for now, with cool clean feet! Further, the devil does not offer a gift for Jesus' feet; he offers only a misguided suggestion about his ministry, about how to protect his feet. Jesus rejects the advice, and goes on – not to broken bones, oddly enough, but to the crucifixion.

Abraham's pattern includes bowing, but Abraham's obeisance is a matter of service, not an arrangement of the hierarchy. Abraham bows out of love, not fear, nor even to acknowledge a greater power. Jesus intends to bow later in his ministry – out of love, not to explain who's boss. The pattern that Abraham establishes and that Jesus embraces is not about power; it's about hospitality: the host bows to the guest, with love and respect. So when the devil suggests that Jesus bow to him, he has missed the point of bowing, completely. When the devil promises to make others bow to Jesus, the Lord has no interest in that whatsoever; on the contrary, he intends to bow to them (us). Further, Jesus does indeed intend that we worship him, but he is completely committed to winning our worship as a free offering; he does not want it forced from us. The devil errs even further, making the offer of worship (and love) conditional: if you do this, I'll do that. By contrast, Jesus offers love unconditionally, and intends to win our unconditional love.

One can argue that Jesus offers hospitality as a reward to us, and so – since rewards are conditional -- the offer is conditional. That is, if we welcome strangers, then God will reward us; and it we refuse hospitality to strangers, he will punish us. That's not complete silliness, but it's not exactly right either. The stranger at the door comes to us as God; when we welcome the stranger, we welcome God. We choose to have a relationship of respect with a stranger, and therefore with God. The relationship that we choose carries over into the next life, where it is much more obvious that such a relationship is an eternal joy. But that's not "conditional"; it's just an explanation of how the thing works. That is, if you do A, and then B happens, we might surmise that A caused B. But that surmise may be an error; it's equally plausible that A is the flip side of B; you do A, then realize that it includes B. That's not cause and effect; it may be, rather, a growing realization of how A and B fit together. Apples don't taste sweet *because* you eat them; they taste sweet, and you notice it when you eat them.

In Matthew 25, Jesus says that if you welcome strangers, you will be welcome in the heaven, and if you don't, you won't. That certainly sounds like a quid pro quo, but it isn't. Rather, it is about entering into a new world of freedom and of free giving. If you enter a world of freedom and love, then ... well, then you are in a world of freedom and love. When you entered the kingdom, you saw a stranger; but once you are in it, you see more clearly that the stranger is an angel. That's not cause-and-effect; it's just growing clarity.

The way that you know you can accept God's forgiveness is that you offer it to others – eagerly, because of course! When you can't help but forgive, God is at work in you, and you are able to accept the immense gifts he offers, including forgiveness.

Imagine a gardener figuring out a pipe. If you put water in this end, it will squirt water out that end. That's true. But to think of it as causality is a little odd. The gardener understands it better: of course water will come out that end if I put water in this end – unless the pipe is clogged with dirt. Causality becomes interesting when you start looking for the dirt in the pipe: water doesn't flow out because there's a rag in the way, or a dead mouse, or maybe just a lot of silt. No one wants an explanation of why water goes through pipes; that's a given. When water gets stuck in the pipe, we want an explanation of that – why water got stuck in the broken hose, and how to fix it. Similarly, we might find it hard to accept forgiveness if we haven't experienced forgiveness flowing through us to others. But this is a matter of problem and solution, not cause and effect.

If you do this, I'll do that, says the devil. That's a deal, not a gift. The devil offers a deal, not hospitality. And it's a kind of deal that Jesus rejects firmly elsewhere: if you do something good for someone else, and that person reciprocates, why is that noteworthy? Even the pagans do that!

The devil did not understand Jesus – nor anything about hospitality.

Chapter 9: The Lamb of God

Among the first steps that Jesus took when he began his ministry was to go to John the Baptist, where John was baptizing. John saw him, and pointed him out: "Behold, the Lamb of God!" (Jn 1:36). What in the world did he mean by that?

Lambs are innocent. They are symbols of spring, and of new life. And they are food, tender and fat.

The Mass recalls two events from the life of Abraham: his hospitality to God and two angels at Mamre, the First Feast, and also the near-sacrifice of Isaac. Abraham believed that the covenant he entered into with God had to be sealed with blood, and in fact he heard God ask for the sacrifice of his son. He went to Moriah to sacrifice his only son. God interrupted before Abraham plunged the knife into Isaac; but the covenant was indeed sealed with the blood of a firstborn – Jesus, the only begotten Son of God – who is indeed Abraham's descendant or "son." Abraham wasn't totally wrong about the sacrifice; he misunderstood a detail.

On the way to Moriah, Isaac asked his father about the sacrifice: where is the sheep? Centuries later, we finally get the answer. When John pointed out the "Lamb of God," and when we recall his words at Mass, the word evokes the memory of Moriah. This is the lamb for the sacrifice, finally.

The event at Moriah was a sacrifice, not an example of hospitality. And yet, Abraham is *also* the prototype of hospitality. And Jesus the sacrificial lamb is *also* food for our deepest self. He offers himself to us as the center of the feast.

The Mass recalls the Passover. The night before the Hebrews left Egypt, they smeared blood on the doorposts and lintels of their homes, so that the angel of God who was going through the land striking down all the firstborn would skip over that house. And then they ate the lamb. The bloody mark of safety was also the center of the feast. John's words recall the Passover lamb: Jesus is the lamb of the new Passover – a sacrifice, not an example of hospitality. And yet, the Passover is celebrated with hospitality. It's sacrificial hospitality.

In one of the "Songs of the Suffering Servant," the one we read every Good Friday, Isaiah describes a mysterious figure who becomes a scapegoat. Scapegoats are described in Leviticus, as part of a ritual to atone for sin. Scapegoats are not killed; they are driven into the wilderness, taking away the sins of the community (Lev 16:5-10). Isaiah's suffering servant "was pierced for our sins, crushed for our iniquity. He bore the punishment that makes us whole, by his wounds we were healed." The Suffering Servant is a sheep, not a goat, but the idea is still there: "We had all gone astray like sheep, all following our own way; but the Lord laid upon him the guilt of us all." (Isaiah 53) Sending the scapegoat (scape-sheep) into the wilderness is a form of sacrifice. And yet, it is also about hospitality – or inhospitality – to a mysterious figure at the edge of the community. The scapegoat serves us, somehow; can we recall him with respect? Can we welcome him back, with honor?

At Mass, when Catholics recall the words of John the Baptist, we add a line immediately about hospitality: "Behold the Lamb of God, behold him who takes away the sins of the world. Blessed are they who are called to supper of the Lamb." The lamb takes away sins: savior. Blessed are they invited to this feast: host. At Mass, the lamb is a symbol of sacrifice and hospitality, both.

Chapter 10: Galilee of the Gentiles

In his monumental work, *Jesus of Nazareth*, Pope Benedict XVI makes a quiet point about the ministry of Jesus: "Matthew immediately follows the story of Jesus' temptation with a short account of the beginning of his ministry. In this context, he explicitly presents Galilee as 'Galilee of the Gentiles' ... the Savior does not come from Jerusalem or Judea, but from a district that was actually regarded as half pagan."

Not Jewish, not pagan: a border between.

When Pope Francis visited Mexico in February 2016, he went to Juarez, across the Rio Grande from El Paso. He celebrated Mass there, a few hundred yards from the border, and he went up a ramp to look across from Mexico to the USA. He went there to dramatize the stupidity and evil of the bitter border, to call us into a renewed determination to restore the unity of the Body of Christ. Jesus Christ stretches across the border: what's our problem?

And that's where Jesus began his ministry, in the community of Juarez-El-Paso. Or Galilee of the Gentiles, a border.

I do not understand the passages in which Jesus states clearly that his ministry was limited – when he said, for example, "I was sent only to the lost sheep of the house of Israel." I think I understand a little about why God chose a specific (and highly articulate) people for himself. Words change their meanings from one generation to the next, and a message that is clear now can be smudged later. For example, when St. Paul's Cathedral was rebuilt after the Great Fire of London, people said the new structure was "awful" and "artificial." The language has changed; 350 years ago, those were words of high praise, meaning "awesome" and "artistic." Stories and parables are much more durable than individual words, but they too are subject to the ravages of time. Consider, for example, references to Sodom: for a thousand years, Sodom was an image of arrogant luxury and injustice, but now people use the story to refer to sexual abuse. Whatever the story means, it is interesting that the perceived meaning changed so much. So I think it matters that God revealed himself in and through a whole culture, which clarifies stories, which in turn clarify words. If you can recover and explore the culture in which someone spoke, it's easier to figure out confidently what a story or gesture or image means. For example, in Jewish culture, if someone says that Jesus rose from the dead, is that a metaphor or a literal claim? Before you start wrestling with whether you believe the story or not, you want to know whether the person who said it, meant it. And there's an answer to that, in the culture. So I'm glad that the Lord chose to speak in and through a culture.

But why did Jesus say he was sent only to the Israelites? I don't know.

I do know that there's a complexity here to explore, an apparent contradiction to unravel. Jesus said that, and then, promptly, did the opposite. He said he was sent to the lost sheep of the house of Israel – and then he healed a Canaanite woman.

He's from Galilee, a border area, half pagan. He's Tex-Mex, from El-Paso-Juarez.

Chapter 11: Educating three leaders

It is not my intention to explain everything that Peter, James, and John learned from Jesus, but simply to look at three passages about them through the lens of hospitality. In Matthew's Gospel, there are three extraordinary passages in which Jesus predicts his passion, and responds to the apostles' near-total failure to understand what he is saying. Three educational incidents:

First. When Jesus asks his disciples who people say he is, they report on what they have heard: John the Baptist, maybe, or Elijah, or a prophet. Then he asks, who do you say I am? Peter responds that he is the Christ, the son of the living God. Jesus approves, and says that Peter has been listening to the Father. But shortly after that, perhaps immediately after that, when Jesus tried to explain what was going to happen in Jerusalem, Peter opposed all this talk of suffering and death. Jesus turned to Peter and said, "Get behind me, Satan! You are an obstacle in my path." (Mt: 16:13-28)

Second. Jesus took Peter, James, and John up a mountain and was transfigured before them. They saw him surrounded by light, conversing with Moses and Elijah. Peter offered to erect three shelters – tents or tabernacles or dwellings, something that provides shade, a *skeinei* or tent. (See the incarnation account in John: the Word became flesh and pitched his tent – in Greek, his *skeinei* – among us; and see also Revelation: "Behold, God's dwelling [*skeinei*, tent] is with the human race. He will dwell [*skenoo*, pitch his tent] with them.") Then a cloud appeared over everything, and a voice came from the cloud: "This is my beloved son; listen to him." (Mt 17:1-13)

Third. The mother of James and John approached Jesus and asked for a favor. She wanted her sons to sit to the right and left of Jesus, in his kingdom. Jesus indicated that he didn't think they had any idea what they were talking about. And then he said, in three ways, that whoever wished to be first should become a servant, imitating the Son of Man. (Mt 20:17-28)

The three scenes with Peter and James and John are associated with three predictions of the Passion. All three passages are extraordinarily rich and complex, but I will skip over almost everything that can be said about them, focusing on one detail: they are interesting from the perspective of hospitality.

The first passage is about the identity of the Lord. Obviously, it matters who he was and is. But suppose we set that question aside for a moment and ask an immediate and practical question: how should people respond to Jesus? From Abraham forward, the proper response to a stranger is to treat him as divine. In this case, Peter treats Jesus as divine, and also thinks he is in fact divine, and also is right. Later, Jesus makes his teaching about strangers explicit: whatever you do for them, you do for me. As you get to know a person, you can explore, learn, discern; but at the outset, in the first encounter, assume you are dealing with God. First impressions matter, and are often quite accurate.

The second passage, about the Transfiguration, is also about the identity of the Lord. But again, there is a secondary matter in the background: how do you make people welcome in the kingdom of God? Peter wanted to capture and hold the moment, to "pickle the peak." He wanted to do something respectful and helpful – and maybe a little noisy. But what he was after, in a clumsy fashion, was an offering of hospitality, like Abraham at Mamre: "Let me provide a place of welcome and rest and shade!" And the voice from the cloud provided a better response, the same advice that Jesus gave to Mary and Martha when Martha was fussing about busy hospitality: "Listen!" That's the heart of hospitality.

The third passage is about how people behave in the kingdom of God. A proud mom wants her sons to get places of prominence. Jesus does not rebuke her, but he does say she doesn't understand. Partly, of course, they don't understand what's going to happen in Jerusalem: the cup that Jesus and his followers will drink is a cup of blood. They are walking toward humiliation and suffering and death. But also, in addition to misunderstanding that the crown of thorns precedes the crown of gold, they still don't understand that the kingdom of God is a kingdom of love and freedom, expressed in service and hospitality. It's not so much that the hierarchy will be upended, with the first going last and the last going first. Nor is it the case that Jesus will preside over a democracy where all are equal. Rather, it's that we are invited into unimaginable, nearly inconceivable, unity with God. When we say: "The Lord be with you," or respond, "And with your spirit," we tend to say it fast, because we can't get our minds around it. It's real! God greets God, with love. And then there's a delightful race to see who will serve whom. When Jesus entered his kingdom, there were a couple of unknown thieves on his right and left hand, and only one of them had any idea whatsoever what was going on. He asked shyly to be remembered, and the Lord showered blessings on him in his humility.

The three lessons about hospitality are not central in these three passages. Not central – but still there. Hospitality was one aspect of what Jesus taught his disciples, just as God taught Abraham about hospitality. Welcome the stranger as you would welcome the Lord; listen attentively; you are invited to share the life of the Trinity.

Chapter 12: Hospitality in John's signs

In his Gospel, John writes about seven "signs" that Jesus used to explain who he is and what he is doing. Scholars do not all use exactly the same list; some items are in dispute. But they include healings and other miracles that explain or justify a series of "I am" claims. Jesus said, "Before Abraham was, I AM," claiming for himself the name that God revealed to Moses. In various places, he said, "I am the vine ... I am the bread of life ... I am the light ... I am the gate ... I am the good shepherd ... I am the way, the truth, and the life." The signs that he gave to justify his "I AM" claims include (following the list that Catholic scholars identify in the notes in the *New American Bible*): (1) the wedding feast at Cana, (2) healing the royal official's son, (3) healing the paralytic at the pool following after the discussion with the woman at the well, (4) the multiplication of loaves and fishes, (5) walking on the water, (6) healing the man born blind, and (7) raising Lazarus from the dead.

Obviously, explaining the signs fully would take the rest of time. The intent here is simply to note that of the seven signs, three involve hospitality.

The wedding feast at Cana (John 2:1-11)
The story of Cana is standard John – extraordinarily dense, with layer after layer of meaning. It's about a wedding: the Lord embraces marriage as fundamental to creation, and to human society, and to revelation. The Bible begins and ends with marriage. And in John's Gospel, the first sign that Jesus gives is at a wedding. Further, the miracle at Cana involves a superabundance of wine: joy poured out unstintingly. Further, Jesus performs the miracle in response to intercessory prayer. Further, it is Mary who intercedes. Further, the sign foreshadows the wine turned to blood at the Last Supper, and the blood poured out on the cross. Further and further, meaning accumulates, quite possibly until the end of time. Three modest points.

At this wedding, the guest was more significant than the host. This feast is probably the best known wedding in human history and literature, but we don't know who the bride and groom were.

We know some of the guests, but not the wedding party. That's bizarre, and delightful, but not necessarily rare. For how many people is it true that the high point of their lives was when they met some great figure, welcomed this figure as guest? The East Coast of the USA has a number of old houses whose claim to fame is that "George Washington slept here." (Some of the claims are probably true.) The Lord offers this experience to all of us, daily (and reliably).

Second, there's a little confusion about who's host and who's guest. When the servants who drew the water, perhaps 150 gallons of water, witnessed the miracle, Jesus sent them off to report to the head waiter. The head waiter concluded, not unreasonably, that the wine was from the groom, because the groom was the host and was therefore – presumably – the source of the wine. That's a delightful bit of confusion, and may have led to jokes and laughter for the next few weeks (or years, or generations). But it is also common: at the doorway, when guests are coming in, it is happens often – not always but often – that there's some discussion, almost argument, about who's more pleased to see whom – who gives more delight in the visit, who takes more delight. And, indeed, is there a real difference between giving and taking delight? The host-guest relationship is like marriage, in the sense that in both relationships, the difference between the giver and the receiver often disappears. Who's lover? Who's beloved? If I give you a bottle of wine and you smile, who got the better gift? So: at the wedding feast in Cana, there was some host-guest confusion – or, more accurately perhaps, some host-guest unity.

Third, guests bring amazing things tucked quietly inside themselves. Jesus was unobtrusive and gentle. The head waiter didn't notice what he did. On that day, at least, the focus was on the bride and groom, and when the Lord of the universe showed up as a guest, he didn't demand attention. Anyone who paid attention to this guest stumbled unawares into the central event of history; but the inattentive missed out on an incredible opportunity. This experience from Cana is also common: every stranger and guest is a mystery, offering new insights and new experiences and new perspectives, with incredible prodigality.

Living water (John 4:4 to 5:18)

The second instance of hospitality in the signs comes in three pieces: the story of the woman at the well, followed by the healing of the royal official's son, leading up to the healing of the paralytic at the pool. The first part is a story of hospitality, the second a story of healing, and the third a story of healing hospitality. The stories are complex, but the lessons about hospitality are accessible.

The incident of the woman at the well unfolds in Samaria. The Jews and the Samaritans were not at war, but they weren't at ease with each other either. A Jew passing through Samaria was an outsider. So when Jesus asks a Samaritan woman at the well for a drink, he is asking her to provide hospitality to a stranger.

In the exchange between the two, Jesus says he can provide living water, and she challenges him to do so. He indicates that he can show her how to be free of her sinful past, and learn to pray. She is impressed, and summons her neighbors, who see the same living wisdom that she saw and conclude that he is indeed the Messiah. So the conversation that started with her as hostess providing water to a stranger turned into a general confession and a new discipleship, in which Jesus provided her with new life and growth – living water.

After the incident of hospitality in Samaria, Jesus returns to Galilee, where he works a visible wonder, healing the son of an official. The connection between the two incidents is not explicit, but it is plausible to link the two in a familiar pattern from Moses: hospitality and salvation. Moses named his sons *Gershom* and *Eliezer*, names that recall hospitality and rescue. These are the two lessons that Moses drew from the Exodos: God saves us from slavery, and we should welcome strangers. And in the desert, God led his people through the Red Sea, then fed his people with bread from heaven. So in John's Gospel, in the signs, Jesus gives living water to the Samaritan woman, and then returns to Galilee and takes the next step in the dance: he heals.

The next incident (the third piece of one sign?) is at the pool of Bethesda. Jesus speaks to a man who has been there for years, hoping to get into the water when it is stirred, when it may heal. But pool has never worked out for the man. Jesus, who is the true living water, heals him. In the previous two incidents, he *gave* living water, and then healed. Here, he *is* the living water, and he heals.

The multiplication of the loaves

The incident of hospitality is also one element of a pair that recalls Moses. The fifth of John's seven signs is feeding 5,000 people with five loaves and two fish – like God feeding his people in the desert. And the sixth sign is walking on the water, demonstrating his control over nature, including water – as God did at the Red Sea. John does not link the two incidents together explicitly, but Mark does. Mark recounts the two incidents together; and at the end of the water story, he says, "They [the disciples] were astounded. They had not understood the incident of the loaves. On the contrary, their hearts were hardened." In other words, if they had understood the miraculous feeding, they would have known that this was the same person who fed the Israelites in the desert, and so – extrapolating logically – of course he would be able to open the Red Sea or walk on the water. This the Lord who works wonders of hospitality and salvation.

Chapter 13: Hospitality smorgasbord (Luke)

Chapters 9 through 11 in Luke's Gospel offer a dozen lessons about hospitality.

1. Jesus sends out the 12 apostles to preach – as strangers who depend on hospitality (Lk 9:1-6)

Take nothing for the journey.
When Jesus sent his apostles to proclaim the kingdom of God and heal the sick, he did not ask them to *welcome* strangers. Rather, he asked them to *become* strangers – beggars or pilgrims on the road, dependent for food and shelter on the hospitality of the people in the towns and villages they visited. It is perhaps noteworthy that Jesus spoke of the *hospitality of individuals*, telling the apostles to stay in whatever house they first entered; but he spoke of the *inhospitality of towns*, telling them how to act when they are not made welcome. That is, the grave wrong of inhospitality is *social* evil, not just an individual sin. When rejected, they were to leave the town – not a house, but the town – and shake the dust from their feet as evidence against them. The evidence of inhospitality is that their feet weren't cleaned: they still had dust on them, because the town didn't provide even the most rudimentary gestures of hospitality.

2. The multiplication of the loaves is a miracle of hospitality, recalling God feeding his people in the desert and foreshadowing the Eucharist. (Lk 10-17)

Send the people away!
When the apostles returned from their mission, the people (who had provided hospitality) followed after them, looking for Jesus. As the long day drew near the end, the apostles urged Jesus to send the people away to find food and lodging. But Jesus asked them to feed the hungry themselves. They said they couldn't; they didn't have enough food for more than a few people. Jesus had the five thousand people sit down, then blessed the five loaves and two fish, broke them in pieces, and distributed them.

When everyone had eaten their fill, they collected the scraps – one basketful per doubting apostle.

3. The transfiguration of Jesus is an image of hospitality. (Lk 9:28-36)

Suddenly there were two men talking to him.
The transfiguration is a glimpse of heaven, and there are a million things to say about it. Three small details:

The three witnesses did not see Jesus charging off to battle bestride the wind, nor sitting on a throne judging, nor receiving and bestowing gifts of gold; rather, they saw an interesting conversation. They saw Jesus' face and clothing change, and take on glory. They saw him conversing with the two men who represent the Law and the Prophets – Moses the Law-Giver and Elijah the great Prophet – speaking of what was to happen in Jerusalem.

Moses, who lived as a stranger in Egypt, led God's people out of that strange land. Elijah too was a stranger – the sojourner from Tishbe. Jesus was not a stranger; he was the King of the Jews (and the universe). But he had been rejected and abused as an unwelcome stranger when he came to his own people in his own land. So the transfiguration was a meeting of three men with a history of being treated as strangers.

Peter's response to the experience is to offer hospitality: let me provide shade and shelter for three. The offer was heartfelt, but ignorant. As Peter was stumbling over his words, a cloud overshadowed them, and they heard the voice of God getting directly to the heart of hospitality: "This is my Son, the Chosen One. Listen to him."

4. Who is the greatest? (Lk 9:47-48)

Anyone who welcomes this little child in my name, welcomes me.
When the apostles went out preaching, they found that they were able to cast out demons and heal people. Often, they were accepted into people's homes and treated respectfully. It seems that they found this intoxicating. In any case, we read, they began to argue about who was greatest. Jesus responded by talking

about hospitality. He doesn't want them thinking they are great because people treat them with respect; that's wrong-headed and upside down. People who treat the apostles with respect are not necessarily doing so because the apostles themselves are great. Jesus sets a child by his side, who – presumably – is not regarded with great respect. And he says, "Whoever receives [gives hospitality to] this child in my name receives me, and whoever receives me receives the one who sent me." People treat the apostles with respect out of respect for the Lord; Jesus could swap an apostle out, replace him with a child, and get the same effect. The apostles should try to be as transparent as possible, so that people can see and know the Lord in and through them.

5. Should the inhospitable village be destroyed like Sodom? (Lk 9:51-56)

Do you want us to call down fire from heaven and burn them up?

In one Samaritan village, James and John smelled out some inhospitality. The village was not pleased or impressed about having a Jew pass through on the way to Jerusalem, and they were not going to provide a welcome. The brothers suggested wiping the town off the face of the earth, with fire. Where did they get such a horrible idea? One possibility is that they recalled an ancient feud, a confrontation between a king of Samaria and the prophet Elijah. The king was hurt in an accident, and sent messengers to get advice from a false god. Elijah intercepted the messengers and asked why they were doing such a thing. When the king heard that Elijah was raising questions, he sent 50 soldiers to fetch him. Elijah summoned fire from heaven to come down and consume the soldiers. This happened twice before Elijah agreed to go see the king. James and John had seen Elijah on a mountaintop recently, so maybe that's where the idea came from. But another possibility is that they recalled what happened when the people of Sodom were inhospitable to a couple of important visitors. Maybe the inhospitable Samaritan town should be Sodom-ized.

6. **The disciples of Jesus may become homeless strangers. (Luke 9:57-58)**

I will follow you wherever you go.
Immediately after the incident with an inhospitable village, Jesus and his followers meet a man who wants to join them. But Jesus warns him that his disciples are dependent on others for hospitality. They do not just *honor* strangers; they *are* strangers. Sometimes being homeless works out, but sometimes it doesn't. "Foxes have dens and birds of the sky have nests, but the Son of Man has nowhere to rest his head."

7. **After the 12 returned with experiences and questions, Jesus sent out 72, with advice about hospitality. (Lk 10: 1-12)**

It will be more tolerable for Sodom on that day than for that town.
When Jesus sent out an expanded group to preach and prepare, he gave instructions that were much like his words to the 12. He explained that they would be vulnerable, like sheep among wolves. He repeated his words about depending on hospitality, and expanded on it. This time, he was explicit about linking inhospitality to the fate of Sodom. If they were not made welcome, they should shake off the dust and leave – confident that God would do justice. Jesus did not take up the suggestion from James and John to burn the cities down right away; but he did say that a day would come for judgment, and on that day, the town would be punished – worse than Sodom.

8. **Define "neighbor."**
When Jesus summed up the whole Law briefly, he was not doing something new and shocking; others had tried to sum up the Law neatly and succinctly. Since his time (and maybe before?), students and scholars and rabbis have challenged each other to "recite the whole Law while standing on one foot." This is not an athletic contest, but a mental exercise: sum it up fast! So, what mattered was not that he summed up the Law succinctly, but how: love God with everything you have, and love your neighbor as yourself. And it was appropriate for the person who was

playing this game to press for some explanation of the word "neighbor." Jesus' explanation of the word has remained challenging ever since.

To understand his explosive approach, it may be worthwhile to explore what the scholar who was testing him might have heard. It was an interesting answer even before Jesus blew up all the boundaries and limitations. The second command that Jesus mentions is in the Law (Leviticus 19:18), but it doesn't stand out in any obvious way. That whole chapter, Leviticus 19, includes a list of relationships that we should tend: with God, parents, the nation, the poor, strangers, hired workers, the deaf and blind, the weak and the powerful, your own family, your siblings – and neighbors. Out of the list of relationships in this chapter, Jesus took one. Why? It's plausible that the word he chose is inclusive of all the others. *Perhaps he used that obscure word because it includes both family and strangers*, with or without various strengths or weaknesses. The word may or may not be as broad enough to include the whole nation. The scholar's question is reasonable, and the answer was interesting even before Jesus transformed the term.

9. The great link between Moses and Jesus on hospitality: Good Samaritan story (Lk: 10:29-37)

This passage is discussed above, in Chapter 3, about continuity. To summarize:

Moses was interested in the division between the Hebrews, descended from Abraham, and the people who lived among them, with roots elsewhere – native-born versus strangers. He commanded that strangers be treated equally, or even receive preferential treatment. The reason for this, he said, was that we can remember what their problems are like: we too, once, were strangers in a strange land. *Remember, and sympathize.* Jesus was interested in the same challenge, or almost exactly the same – although he approached the problem from a slightly different perspective. Where's the line between "neighbors" whom we should love, and non-neighbors we can neglect? Jesus said there is no such legal boundary. The only limitation is in our imaginations. Put yourself in the place of someone in need. If you can imagine the need, you should help. *Imagine, and sympathize.*

10. Martha and Mary offer hospitality: listen or serve? (Lk 10:38-42)

Please tell her to help me.

When Jesus visited Martha and Mary, the sisters both offered hospitality, but in different ways. Mary sat and listened, while Martha raced around doing all the chores of serving. When Martha complained, Jesus defended Mary's choice. For sure, service matters; but listening is better. It's not hard to imagine the scene, nor to sympathize with Martha's complaint; but Jesus makes clear that what matters most in hospitality is an open and listening heart.

The controversial 14th century German mystic and theologian, Meister Eckhart, OP, says that we should be careful to avoid a false dichotomy, service versus listening. He says that Martha may have been listening and also serving, while Mary was just listening. So, Eckhart argues, Martha was doing better than Mary. But Jesus defends the weaker sister, saying that Mary has started well, choosing to learn first how to do what matters most. Give her time, and she too will learn to listen and serve at the same time. Whether Eckhart has it right or not, it is surely true that hospitality matters greatly, and that the heart of it is careful attention to the needs of the guest, whatever those needs are.

Madonna House, a community of service and prayer founded by Catherine de Hueck Doherty, provides hospitality in small houses around the world. They have soup kitchens and clothing exchanges. But they believe that greatest hunger in many parts of the world is not for food, but for love – and more specifically, for an attentive audience, for a sympathetic and interested ear. They listen, as an act of hospitality.

11. Our Father: hospitality and salvation (Lk 11:1-4)

Give us each day our daily bread, and forgive us our sins.

Every word and phrase and inflection of this prayer has been used and scrutinized for centuries. One detail: this prayer taught by the Lord includes the two-part prayer of Moses.

The prayer begins offering love and worship to God, but then turns to specific requests for our sake. The requests are (or include) hospitality and salvation. First: "Give us this day our daily bread." Certainly, this prayer includes a reference to knowing the truth, or learning to serve; but at root it is a prayer that God will meet our basic needs – will be hospitable to us. Second is a prayer that God forgive us. The prayer includes some clarity about how forgiveness works: we will not be able to accept forgiveness if we don't participate in it, forgiving others. But at root, it is a prayer that God will save us from the forces within us that can destroy us forever. That is, putting the two together, we ask our Father to be, for us, a Lord and host who feeds us and meets our daily needs, and also savior who frees us from sin.

Moses taught that we should remember the experience of slavery in Egypt. Remembering, we should respond in two ways: thank God for rescuing us from slavery, and welcome strangers because we can sympathize.

12. Prayer and hospitality in the night (Lk 11:5-13)

Friend, lend me three loaves of bread.
Jesus says that in our prayer, we should be persistent. The example that he gives is about hospitality. More specifically, it's about putting together the ability to serve with the heart to serve. It's a struggle: persevere.

A neighbor shows up in the middle of the night, asking for help providing hospitality to a third person, an unexpected midnight guest at his house. The guest should be made welcome, of course, which means that he should find an open heart (done) and shelter (done) and something to eat (not done). So the host goes next door to beg. The host has the disposition to serve; the neighbor has the ability. The man with a heart to serve persists until he gets bread for his guest. And he succeeds, not because the sleepy neighbor embraces the call to hospitality that the unprepared host feels, but because the neighbor wants to go back to sleep, and can't until he cooperates.

It is not common to wake up in the middle of the night because a neighbor is banging on the door, begging. Or perhaps more precisely: this event is not common if we are specific and literal about it. It is indeed common to wake up in the middle of the night aware of a need, troubled by a problem, wrestling with an internal call to action.

The midnight call to clarity and action is, perhaps, God at the door. Oddly, that makes God the one who is praying while we listen reluctantly. Who's host, and who's guest, in that scene? Perhaps the Lord's description of prayer is yet another example of how the host-guest relationship is often (always?) ambiguous, with the host and guest swapping places constantly.

Jesus is confident that if we pray persistently, we will get results. His examples are both about food: we will get fish and eggs, not snakes and scorpions. But his real point is about a far greater gift: if we persist, God will give us his Holy Spirit. Which includes the heart to serve, and the ability, both. And a lot more.

At Mamre, when Abraham offers hospitality to three strangers, the pattern of hospitality culminates in the gifts given by the guests. God promises Abraham that he will be the father of many nations. What Jesus talks about here is even greater: if you enter this relationship – this exchange of gifts that we call hospitality – with God, he will not be outdone in generosity. He will give you his Holy Spirit.

13. Hospitality to Satan (Lk 11:14-26)

I shall return to my home from which I came.

Luke recounts that Jesus drove a demon out of a man, and then had some discussion about the event. The discussion includes three binary choices, two about hospitality.

Jesus' critics suggest that he might be driving out demons by the power of a greater demon. Jesus says that doesn't make sense, for two reasons: (1) how can hell get anything done if it's divided, and (2) if Jesus drives out demons by the power of other demons, how do the leaders of the community ever drive out demons? So, he says, you have to choose what to believe: if the demons are being driven out by the finger of God, then the kingdom of God is at hand. Choose!

Second, Jesus says that if you don't gather with him, you scatter. The word he uses for "gather" is *synago* – to collect or sweep together. It's what hens do with chicks, what fishermen do with fish – and it's what the Lord demands that we do with strangers. The verb takes an object: when someone says he is gathering, the ear waits to hear what is being gathered. What is Jesus gathering? Elsewhere in the New Testament, people gather wheat, fish, friends for prayer, nations for judgment, and strangers. Which is this? On the other hand, the word for "scatter" is *skorpizo* – an unpleasant word, a cognate for the noun *scorpion*. It's what wolves do to sheep if the good shepherd isn't there. Are you a hospitable person, or a scorpion? Choose!

The third choice is a sober reason for cooperating with Jesus when he gathers whatever or whomever he wants gathered. After a demon is driven out, it may wander through the wastelands, then return with friends. If the demon returns, the only way to keep it out is by having your palace guarded by a strong man, stronger than the demons. So you will make room in your palace – your heart, your life – for Jesus and whomever he collects, or for demons and whomever they collect. Freely or under compulsion, you will open your door. To whom? Choose!

14. Sign of Jonah: repentance. Strangers did, from Nineveh (location unclear) and Queen of the South

It is worth noting that the "sign of Jonah" refers to a message that foreigners got, but the native-born did not. Jonah went to Nineveh (location a little unclear, since it seems to be approximately 100 miles inland, on a coast – but anyway, not in Judea) and preached repentance. The people heard him, and repented. Continuing the thought, Jesus mentions the Queen of the South (location a little unclear, but not in Judea) who came to hear the wisdom of Solomon. Strangers listened; Hebrews did not. Jesus calls attention to the reach of his message – to his own people, but also to foreigners.

The teaching about hospitality in these three chapters is startlingly rich and abundant. It isn't focused, isn't immediately and obviously applicable to modern squabbles about immigration policy. But the idea that there's nothing in Scripture about the modern issue – or nothing in the New Testament – is ludicrous. It's all over the place!

Aside: Thomas Aquinas on washing feet

In general, I see hospitality and forgiveness as two key aspects of the work of the Lord. Jesus is Lord – not in pomp and majesty, but like a host at a feast. And Jesus is savior – re-assembling the smashed pieces of our hearts, souls, cities, societies. And I think of washing feet as a detail of hospitality.

Thomas Aquinas sees it differently. In his Commentary on the Gospel of St. John, in his third lecture on chapter 13, Aquinas talks about washing feet. At the Last Supper, which parallels the First Feast at Mamre, Jesus washes the feet of his disciples, imitating Abraham's care of his visitors. Washing feet – or at least providing water to wash – is a standard detail of Biblical hospitality. But Aquinas, examining the passage, focuses instead on forgiveness.

Aquinas says that the Lord's actions at the Last Supper leave us with a serious obligation to wash each other's feet; in fact, he argues, it is a grave evil not to do so (qui negligit praeceptum peccat mortaliter). It's best to do it physically, literally, he says – but if we can't do it physically, we can and must do it in our hearts. In his view, this metaphorical wash means washing away sin – by forgiveness and prayer (which anyone can do, and all must do), and by the sacrament of Reconciliation (a priest's role).

Aquinas argues that when the Lord washed the disciples' feet, he was gesturing toward all the works of mercy – feeding the hungry, clothing the naked, and welcoming visitors.

Aquinas sees the act of washing feet, at least metaphorically or spiritually, as a grave obligation. And he sees this act as forgiveness and hospitality, both.

Chapter 14: First Feast and Last Supper

The example of Abraham's hospitality to strangers can deepen our understanding of the Last Supper.

Jesus upends the story about Abraham. In Genesis, man welcomes God and his angels. In the Gospel, the Son of God is host to mankind.

The Last Supper includes details that are familiar from the story of Abraham: washing the feet of guests, a feast, bread, startlingly assertive hospitality, deadly serious business afterwards.

When the three strangers appear at his tent, Abraham hastens to welcome them, and offers them water to wash their feet. Jesus changes this a little: he not only provides water, but washes their feet himself. Peter balks at this, but Jesus insists. Then Peter agrees to permit the Lord to wash his feet; but says that if the Lord is going to wash him, then really he should wash everything – and Jesus balks.

The feast that Abraham provides is roast beef and cheese, with milk. The feast that Jesus arranges is a Passover feast, so one can presume that it included lamb and vegetables, with wine.

Abraham provided fresh bread. Jesus provided living bread.

Abraham welcomed strangers. What Jesus arranged was for his friends, not strangers; nonetheless, it is clear that he offered boundless hospitality. When you welcome a stranger, you take a risk: the stranger may be unpleasant, or disruptive, or even dangerous. Jesus did not take *risk*: with his eyes open, he provided a welcome for Judas. Judas was about to betray him to death, and still Jesus made him welcome.

After the feast, Abraham went outside and bargained with God, asking him to spare the city where his nephew dwelt. He asked, "Will you really sweep away the righteous with the wicked?" He asked God to have mercy for the sake of 50 just men. How about 45? 40? 30? 20? Ten? God listened to him, and agreed – but there weren't ten to be found. The next day, in Sodom, the angels invite Lot, his wife, his daughters, and their husbands. Six. The husbands laugh it off. Four. Lot's wife leaves town, but looks back. Three. Lot and two daughters survive, and everyone else is killed.

After the Last Supper, Jesus makes clear that he understands how many just men there are in Jerusalem. He predicts that Peter, the Rock, will betray him that night. Jesus talks to his Father, and re-affirms the plan. The only just man will die, so everyone else can live.

Hospitality is a single facet of these complex stories. But the words of Jesus (in Luke's Gospel) add another insight into hospitality. At one point during dinner, some of the apostles argue about who is foremost among them. Jesus responds, talking about his kingship – not as a matter of power and pomp and prestige, but as a celebration. The king will be host at a feast; and, Jesus reminds them, "I am among you as one who serves." Like Abraham.

Understanding Mamre matters, shedding light on the Last Supper.

Chapter 15: Hospitality and the Trinity

Hospitality is one ray of light straight from the heart of the Triune God.

In my book Straight Guilt *I looked at a list of seven images that we use to begin trying to understand the life of the Trinity. The following material is swiped from that book, and slightly re-worked.*

It seems to me that the world reflects the glory of God, and so anyone with a mind or a heart is invited to discover God. So if God is triune – Father and Son united by the Spirit – then we will see that fundamental reality reflected in the universe and in our experiences. Some images help; others don't. Four examples follow.

First image: the shamrock
There's a story that St. Patrick compared the Trinity to a shamrock. I don't believe it. It is possible that he (or a follower) suggested that we can recall God whenever we see three leaves. That would trigger a lot of prayer. But did he use it as an image to explain and enlighten? I just don't believe that. It's a silly go-nowhere image, worse than useless. I have never heard anyone pick up that image and then take another step. When people start with the shamrock, what they say next is that the Trinity is a mystery and we can't understand it. But Catholic "mysteries" are invitations to infinite depth, not obedient excursions down a dead end! I like shamrocks; I like tough pride growing everywhere; I like green. But shamrocks don't explain the Trinity. To engage the brain, we need something else. And other images abound.

Second image: 1 + 1 = 3
In literature and all successful art, one plus one is at least three, often much more. That is, when you juxtapose two items artfully, you get item #1 plus item #2 – plus #3, the magic or comparison or story that emerges between the two.
A haiku, for example, may juxtapose two images to express a feeling that is intense and specific, but has never been captured in

a single word. The picture of a bird balancing on a strand of barbed wire includes two items, the bird and the wire. But the juxtaposition may stir up ideas about freedom, about flight, about the futility of trying to imprison the heart.

Consider a poem of William Carlos Williams:

> It's a strange courage
> you give me, ancient star;
> shine alone in the sunrise
> toward which you lend no part.

Williams (and I) find that the juxtaposition of a single star (probably the planet Venus, actually) and a dramatic sunrise can stir deep feelings that are separate from the star or the sunrise. Williams points toward the feeling – "courage" – but promptly asserts that this word is only an approximation: it's a "strange courage." Dare to be great: sure, sure, but I'm not. Then dare to be small and independent and fiery and beautiful on your own terms!

All art operates by juxtaposition and/or contrast. The magic emerges between items, not within an item. And this familiar magic is, I think, an image of the Trinity. Or perhaps I should say, it's an invitation to notice a million images of the life of the Trinity. And that's why it is so hard to find anyone who starts with the legend of Patrick's shamrock and goes on to say something insightful about the Trinity. The Trinity is not about three branches of government; it's about the Father and the Son – and the unifying Relationship between them.

It's not just art – not art alone – that proceeds by juxtaposition, this minor variation on the life of the Trinity. All science does also. When a snowflake is taking shape, you have a water molecule here and a water molecule there – and the extraordinarily delicate balance of charges that creates symmetry. The pairs, and the Gentle Tug Toward Symmetry, create trillions and quadrillions of beautiful variations.

Another: the Fibonacci series in mathematics (each number is the sum of the previous two) describes the growth of living things better than simple doubling. That is, if you think that cells just double and double – 1, 2, 4, 8 – you are left without a handle on how cells slowly change and specialize; the two cells from each doubling should be identical. But since cells actually grow by a different series – 1, 1, 2, 3, 5, 8, 13 – each cell has its own unique history, its own unique lineage – and indeed then its own unique place in the growing organism. The first hint of this mathemagic is the 3. When we get two cells, they don't just start from scratch and double again; something happens between the cells.

The relationship matters. 1 + 1 = 3.

The clearest image: marriage

It seems to me that the simplest and most common human experience that reveals the life of the Trinity is marriage. Two people become one: that's an intensely exciting, endlessly fascinating, usually challenging perplexity. The relationship that unifies the two – that makes them "one" – is extraordinary in many ways, including its external fecundity. That is, we often – not always, but often – observe the exciting progression from a relationship straight through to the birth of a child. There are discernible and significant events and decisions along the way; but still, we can trace an unbroken continuity from the relationship to the birth. The relationship which unifies two people and makes them one – the relationship! – goes on to become a third person.

That is, marriage is a clear image of the life of the Trinity – for many people, the clearest image. The relationship between the Father and the Son is a third Person. We can see that happen in time, in a marriage; and we can imagine it in eternity.

In marriage, we can watch the life of the Trinity lived out in time. In freedom, we choose to love each other. In joy, we become one. Not always, but often, our love spills over to produce a child: the relationship becomes a person. But for God, there's no "becoming"; the future is now.

We can know the life of the Trinity most deeply in a marriage. We live it. The future squirms in our arms, making sweet demands now.

Fourth image: hospitality

As an image of the life of the Trinity, hospitality is not as clear as marriage, but it's close.

Scripture says it over and over: when a stranger knocks on your door, you are to welcome that person as if he or she is an angel sent by God. In fact, sometimes the visitor is indeed an angel. Jesus strengthened that idea: he said that the way we greet and treat the stranger at the door is the way we greet and treat God, always. When we are hospitable to a stranger, God accepts this gift as a gift to himself – not sometimes, but always. But then, when God comes to visit, who is host and who is guest? Abraham offered hospitality to God; but before the end of the day, God was in charge, and God was giving gifts.

In the prayer that Jesus taught, the lordship of God is not a matter of power and pomp; it's about a feast in the house of Lord. Give us "our daily bread," we ask. Who gives bread daily? The host at a feast provides the food and drink – at a week-long wedding, or in a life-long community hall like Hrothgar's mead benches in *Beowulf*, or at eternal feast. In the Lord's Prayer and elsewhere, the lordship of Jesus is the lordship of a host at a banquet.

So which one is an image of God: host or guest? Both. God is the guest when we are the host, but the host when we are the guest. That's the way hospitality works.

When an immigrant shows up at the border, one aspect of this encounter is that the Lord himself stands there knocking. Like the angels at Mamre, the stranger is a visitor from heaven, whatever we see at first glance. But also, the proper response is to act as God acts, and in fact to act in the name of God – to be a good host.

The relationship between a host and guest is not a power contest; it's an invitation into a new and rich relationship. That is to say, the speck on the horizon or the knock on the door is an invitation into the life of the Trinity.

The guest/host relationship is an invitation into the mystery of love. Who's host? Once we get accustomed to sharing, who cares? We are bound together. The host and the guest have interchangeable roles. This isn't confusion of identity; it's unity.

Chapter 16: Hospitality in the Eucharist

The celebration of the Eucharist is loaded, from beginning to end, with references to hospitality and examples of the rich relationship between hosts and guests. In this chapter, the intention is not to prove a point, but rather to use previous insights to enjoy a wealth that God has showered on us.

1. Greeting: the Trinity in host/guest relationship

The Mass opens, like nearly all Christian prayer, with the Sign of the Cross – a gesture, a memory, a statement, an invocation. The gesture, drawing a simple cross on our bodies, is an obvious reference to Jesus' self-sacrificial love, giving his life for us, while the words recall the Trinity. Even after decades of practice, anyone who can meditate on the crucifixion and also on the Trinity in the time it takes to make the sign of the cross must be brilliant and/or holy.

In those impossibly brief three or four seconds, though, when we think of the Trinity, it's appropriate to recall that one ray of light from the heart of the Trinity is hospitality. Among the most evocative and beautiful portrayals of the Trinity is the great icon painted by Andrei Rublev, showing the scene at Mamre. The text in Genesis speaks of Abraham welcoming God and two angels. Rublev paints the scene as three figures of immense dignity and peace, sitting together in tranquil love, and he uses the traditional colors of iconography to portray the Father, the Son, and the Holy Spirit. The image is of the Trinity, accepting and bestowing hospitality in Mamre.

2. exchange of blessings

May the Lord be with you. ... And with your spirit.
This simple exchange appears in the Mass at the opening, the Gospel, the beginning of the Eucharistic Prayer, and the dismissal. It's familiar, and slides past fast. But wait a moment: who can invoke the Lord this way, speak such words confidently? These are shocking words! If the Lord hears and grants these prayers, who is host and who is guest in this exchange? This is God,

pleased to be with God. God (dwelling in me, and listening to my prayer) is pleased to see God (dwelling in you, and listening to your prayer). The host and guest are nearly (totally?) indistinguishable.

3. Penitential Act

I confess ... that I have sinned ... in my thoughts and in my words, in what I have done, and in what I have failed to do.

The penitential rite is an extraordinarily odd moment. We gather for a celebration, and then begin by thinking about dirt and muck and awful stuff. "Welcome, welcome, come on in, take off your coat, have a seat, make yourself at home – and then let's talk about grime and horror." Did I hear right? But actually, odd as this rite seems at first glance, I believe it is psychologically precise, exactly the right thing to do. We don't want the memory of our sins rising up to reproach us later on in the celebration, distracting us with the shocking awareness that we do not belong at this celestial event. So right from the start, let's be clear: we are not worthy to be there, but we are invited anyway. We are not worthy, but we are protected by the generosity of the host, who asked us to come. We can stay, because he said so. When we get that part straight – about the host/guest relationship – then we can participate in the celebration with freedom and joy.

But there's another small puzzle. We have sinned in four ways, including a familiar trio of experience – thought, word, and deed. But there's a fourth: omission. The *Catechism of the Catholic Church* discusses sins of omission in two contexts: scandal and euthanasia. But surely, we don't add this fourth category to the penitential rite at every Mass to deal with scandal and euthanasia! So why is it there? Perhaps because the Lord's description of the Last Judgment in Matthew 25 refers to six sins that lead to eternal punishment, and all six mortal sins in the Lord's list are sins of omission.

4. The Liturgy of the Word is food for the soul

The Mass is divided in two parts, the Liturgy of the Word and the Liturgy of the Eucharist. The Liturgy of the Word is an example of God's generosity and hospitality. He feeds us with his Word.

The Second Vatican Council, in the *Constitution on Divine Revelation*, said that "the force and power in the word of God is so great that it stands as the support and energy of the Church, the strength of faith for her sons, the food of the soul, the pure and everlasting source of spiritual life." It is a source of energy and strength – it is both food and drink.

5. Consecration: on the night before he was to suffer

At the consecration, we recall what happened the night before Jesus was to suffer. That is, the words of the consecration invite us to recall the events of Holy Thursday in connection with Good Friday. The feast and the crucifixion are tied together carefully and deliberately. This is about hospitality and salvation, both, woven together inextricably.

The consecration includes the transubstantiation of both bread and wine. We recall the words of the Lord, who said, "Take and eat, for this is my body ... take and drink, for this is my blood." The layers of meaning here go on forever, but one detail is that the Last Supper is rich and overflowing hospitality, like the First Feast at Mamre, and the wedding feast at Cana.

6. Our Father

There are many different ways to explore and understand the structure of the Our Father. For example, some Christians find a wealth in examining the seven requests within it. One aspect of the prayer that the Lord taught us is that it resembles the Ten Commandments: the first half is focused on God, and the second half is still addressed to God but is focused on our needs. And what we ask for is hospitality and salvation. Hospitality: "give us this day our daily bread." Salvation: "forgive us our sins."

The prayer flows logically and coherently: both requests are attached to the adjacent words in obvious ways. When we ask God to give us our daily bread, this comes right after praying, "thy kingdom come, thy will be done on earth as it is in heaven." We believe that his kingdom is a kingdom of generosity and hospitality; and in his kingdom, we are fed. We believe that when his will is done here on earth as it is in heaven, we will see and accept God's hospitality, and we will be conduits of his love and hospitality, so that all of us give and receive the gifts of the kingdom – from God, but also from each other.

When we ask God to forgive us, we add some sobering and challenging words: "forgive us our trespasses as we forgive those who trespass against us." This is not because we take the initiative and God imitates us, nor is God's love conditional on our actions. It is God's initiative, but his forgiving love pours on us *and through us*. If we think we can accept his forgiveness without forgiving others, we have misunderstood him. Love that doesn't go through us, didn't get to us.

7. Lamb of God: we are invited as guests

At communion, the priest holds up the host and says, "Behold the Lamb of God ..." Jesus is the Good Shepherd, and the gate of the sheepfold, and the lamb. He is priest and victim. He dies for us our sins, saving us; and he feeds us, with inexhaustible hospitality.

The priest continues: " ... Happy are those who are called the supper of the Lamb." These words are addressed to those who are invited, the *guests*. It's worth noting this, because our response is that we aren't worthy to be *hosts*.

The people respond to the priest's invitation recalling the words of the centurion, who asked Jesus for a miracle for someone else, but did not ask him to enter his house. The centurion was not an immigrant; but he was an outsider, part of an occupying army. At this moment of God's great offer of hospitality, we identify with an outsider, whose welcome and worthiness are questionable. But then we continue, in-spired and en-couraged by the Church, with the next words of the centurion, slightly amended. The centurion said, "But only say the word, and my servant will be healed." We say, "But only say the word, and my soul shall be healed." Who's worthy to accept the hospitality of the Lord? No one, so forget about that. Who's invited? Everyone who is willing to accept his gifts of healing and hospitality.

Chapter 17: The Last Judgment (Mt 25)

When did we see you a stranger and welcome you?

In Matthew's account, there are two chapters that focus on the destruction of the temple and Jesus' final return. After these two chapters, the gospel moves on the climax of the gospel: the Last Supper and the crucifixion and resurrection of the Lord. The two chapters are stiff and sober, full of warning and advice about preparing for judgment; and the final piece of this section is a description of the Last Judgment, when the Son of Man will judge all the nations of the world, as a shepherd separates the sheep from the goats. The judgment puts each person in one of two groups. "The king will say to those on his right, 'Come, you who are blessed by my Father. Inherit the kingdom prepared for you from the foundation of the world. ... Then he will say to those on his left, 'Depart from me, you accursed, into the eternal fire prepared for the devil and his angels.'" As Jesus describes it, this sorting is based on good – acts of mercy – on one hand; and evil – sins of omission – on the other hand.

Jesus lists six specific acts of mercy, and repeats the list four times. You did these things, he says – and goes through a list of six. People respond with astonishment: when did we do these things – and they repeat the list. Jesus explains, "Whatever you did for one of these least brothers of mine, you did for me." Then Jesus turns to the other group, and charges them with failure. You did not do these things, he says – and repeats the list of six. They too respond with astonishment: when did we fail to do these things – and they too repeat the list. Jesus explains to them, "What you did not do for one of these least ones, you did not do for me." Then the people go off to eternal life or eternal punishment.

One approach to the list is to search out the spirit of the thing. The specific details of people's desperate needs change, depending on time and place and circumstance. The spirit, not the letter, matters. People who develop addictions to drugs or alcohol often have food and water and clothing and shelter, but they need help – so help, in the spirit of that sobering passage. That makes sense to me. The spirit of the passage is quite clear, and perhaps that's sufficient. Still, I'm reluctant to walk away from the list carelessly: Jesus repeated it four times.

The list is sober, significant – and also somewhat odd, by our standards today. In our time, most people who discuss the list skip over the third specific command, about strangers. To our ear, it sounds arbitrary – why not take care of the blind, the lame and the halt? Why not take care of food and clothing and shelter? Actually, that's a common modern translation, replacing "strangers" with "homeless": to our ear, that sounds much smoother. Why "stranger"? I have tried, by reviewing the extensive teaching about hospitality in the Old Testament and the New Testament, to understand this matter, and to answer that question.

Perhaps hospitality to strangers is the fundamental command here, as hospitality is fundamental in the teaching of Moses. Perhaps the list includes: (1) a general command – be hospitable; plus (2) three specific details about hospitality – provide food and water and even clothes if necessary; plus (3) a command to be proactive about hospitality, not only responding to people who knock on our doors with their needs, but also reaching out to people in need who will not come to our doors – the sick and the imprisoned.

If that's the case, then can we paraphrase the list of six in such a way that it seems to flow smoothly from beginning to end? A suggested paraphrase:

"In the end, we will be judged on love, and specifically on our hospitality. When people have basic needs, like food and water, help! But hospitality includes more than life-or-death basics! Meet the needs you see! If someone needs clothes, take care of that too. In fact, seek out people in need, and go to where they are to help – in their sick beds or hospitals or jails!"

The point here is not to provide a clearer teaching, but to provide a presentation that flows from beginning to end with some coherence.

Clothe the naked

There is a challenge in understanding the list that Jesus provides. Jesus said we should feed the hungry, and he did so himself – extravagantly. He said we should give drink to the thirsty, and he did so himself – although in his discussion with the woman at the well, he asks her for water from the well, and provides her with living water. He said we should welcome strangers, and did so beginning in the first weeks of his life with Mary and Joseph. He visited – and healed – the sick. That's four of the six. But did he clothe the naked, or visit the imprisoned?

The fourth work of mercy that Jesus mentions is clothing the naked. Is it likely or even possible that Jesus would demand something of us that he didn't do himself? When did Jesus clothe the naked?

When Jesus was crucified, the soldiers divided his garments by casting lots. But he didn't turn them over willingly, and the soldiers weren't naked. Skip that; that's not living out the six precepts.

We don't read much about Jesus' clothing. He was wrapped in swaddling clothes when he was a baby (Lk 2:7). At the time of his transfiguration, he wore dazzling white (Lk 9:29). But there's no hint that he gave any of that away.

Jesus told stories in which clothes mattered. In the story of the Good Samaritan (Lk 10:29-37), the victim by the side of the road was stripped before he was beaten. That's inhospitality. But there's no mention of the Samaritan replacing the man's clothes.

In the story of the prodigal son (Lk 15: 11-32), when the son returns home, the father welcomes him with a feast, but also orders the servants: "Quickly bring the finest robe and put it on him; put a ring on his finger and sandals on his feet." But the point does not seem to be warmth or protection: he gets the "finest" robe, and a ring. The father dresses his son in dignity.

Perhaps clothing the naked is more metaphorical than literal. In Genesis, Adam and Eve ate the apple, and then discovered that they were naked. There's no obvious connection between apples, or even apple peels, and clothes. St. Pope John Paul II wrote extensively about the meaning of nakedness when he was developing his theology of the body. In "Real Significance of Original Nakedness," he wrote that man had lost "loses the original certainty of the image of God, expressed in his body." His "original acceptance of the body as a sign of the person in the visible world" had collapsed.

Perhaps, sometimes, clothing the naked has little or nothing to do with clothes. Perhaps it's more like St. Francis hearing from God that he should rebuild the church, and starting to fit bricks in place. He worked with bricks and mortar for a while, which wasn't a bad way to start; it took time before he understood that the real work had to do with humanity.

Perhaps the real task that Jesus mentions here is clothing the person in dignity. When Moses provided for widows and orphans and strangers, commanding that landowners leave grapes and grain and olives for the poor, he also commanded that the food be provided in a way that protected the dignity of the gleaners.

Thomas Aquinas, writing about these works of mercy, said that the "spiritual" works of mercy take primacy over the "corporal" works of mercy. Aquinas made the remark about two lists that were not Scripture, although they were based on Scripture. Still, the remark seems a little presumptuous, exalting a medieval theory over the words of Jesus – until you notice that there might be a basis for the remark in Jesus' own list. Clothing the naked may be among the spiritual works of mercy.

Jesus did certainly clothe people in dignity. For example, when the scribes and Pharisees brought a woman to him who had been caught in adultery (Jn 8:1-11), and asked whether she should be stoned, he said to them, "Let the one among you who is without sin be the first to throw a stone at her." They all drifted away. Then he asked her, "Woman, where are they? Has no one condemned you?" When she replied that no one had done so, he said, "Neither do I condemn you. Go, and from now on do not sin anymore." He clothed her in dignity.

When did Jesus visit the imprisoned?

When John was imprisoned, messengers went back and forth between Jesus and John, but there's no hint anywhere that Jesus visited John. Were there any other prisoners – literal prisoners – in the Gospels? Jesus freed us from sin and hell and death, which are much more serious than dungeons. In a sense, living in an occupied land – Palestine in the time of Jesus, or North Korea today – is visiting the imprisoned. But did he visit any prisoners, individuals in lockup somewhere?

The day before he died, he was himself a prisoner. So even if he did not spend time visiting other prisoners, he did make their plight his own. And when he asks us to visit prisoners, he is inviting us to understand a little more about his life. But did he set an example that we can imitate?

The record of his time with another prisoner is about a brief and distracted visit. But it's intense. All the Gospels mention that Jesus was crucified between two criminals or revolutionaries. Luke's account adds a detail, distinguishing between the two men. One of them joined the soldiers and the mob abusing Jesus. But the other defended Jesus: "Have you no fear of God, for you are subject to the same condemnation? And indeed, we have been condemned justly, for the sentence we received corresponds to our crimes, but this man has done nothing criminal."

Whatever others saw in this man, what the Lord saw – or what we hear about when Jesus was with this man – is honesty and courage.

Then the man turned to Jesus and said, "Jesus, remember me when you come into your kingdom." The words include a request – "remember me" – but far more. Everyone around Jesus was shouting and mocking Jesus for thinking he was a king, but this man speaks words of encouragement: he believes that Jesus is on his way to a kingdom. His words are kind and comforting. Further, he urges Jesus to focus on what is to come: that's good advice. Did Jesus *need* people with him during this crisis? No, but he did *want* them; he did ask Peter and James and John to pray with him.

Jesus did not arrange a visit with the warden, and come during visiting hours. Jesus met the man because they got crucified together. But among the last things they did before death was to exchange generous and open-hearted gifts with each other: respect, repentance, solidarity. As with most instances of hospitality, the distinction between host and guest isn't important; what happened was mutual generosity.

It was a joy, deeper than death, to give and receive gifts on their crosses. They each gave something; and each was certainly aware of the other's generosity, and grateful for it. Jesus, of course, gave more: "Today you will be with me in Paradise." The first person to benefit from the cross was this thief.

Was this work of mercy "corporal" or "spiritual"? Clearly both. Mercy is multi-layered.

So, yes: Jesus did visit a prisoner. And it was intense.

Chapter 18: Hospitality after the Resurrection

The three synoptic Gospels describe events after the resurrection briefly, in a chapter apiece. John's Gospel has two post-resurrection chapters. All four have significant teaching about hospitality.

Matthew, chapter 28

Matthew's Gospel does not have any post-resurrection *stories* of hospitality, but the instructions are noteworthy. There is a single chapter reporting the resurrection, the angel's words at the tomb, the experience of Mary Magdalen and the other Mary, the initial reaction of the elders and the Roman soldiers, and then – in five verses – the commissioning of the apostles. The chapter is packed tight, and it is terse. Nonetheless, the words of instruction to the apostles contain seeds of hospitality.

First, the apostles went to Galilee, as instructed, and met the risen Jesus there. This is, as Pope Benedict pointed out, Galilee of the Gentiles, a border land at the edge of Judea, where Jews and non-Jews were intermingled. Jesus spoke to them there, at the periphery, and then sent them beyond the periphery: "Go and make disciples of all nations." Jesus spoke and acted inside a specific culture, so that his words and actions could be understood within an illuminating context. But as soon as his own specific mission was completed, the work of the apostles was promptly extended to the world. He took them to the edge of their homeland, and shoved them beyond. Throughout his life in Palestine, Jesus was a stranger in his own land – native-born, but in an occupied land ruled by Rome and Rome's puppets. The apostles are to spend their lives as strangers in a variety of strange lands. All the world is equally foreign, equally familiar, mission territory.

Second, they are to baptize in the name of the Trinity, an unfathomable mystery of hospitality.

Third, Jesus' final words in Matthew's Gospel recall the name that the angel revealed to Joseph in the opening of Matthew's Gospel. The angel had said, "you are to name him Jesus … they shall name him Emmanuel." The name "Jesus" refers God's action saving us; the name "Emmanuel" means "God is with us." Together, the names can be taken to refer to Jesus as Savior and hospitable Lord, like the names of Moses' two sons Gershom and Eliezer ("be hospitable to strangers" and "God saves.") The Gospel ends with the newly risen Savior claiming the title of hospitality: "And behold, I am with you always, until the end of the age." Emmanuel, to the end of time.

Mark, chapter 16

Mark's Gospel also reports events after the resurrection in a single chapter.

He refers to the women who went to the tomb to anoint the body of Jesus, to offer final gestures of hospitality – not to make the dead man comfortable any more, but nonetheless to show respect and love.

The women were not sure how they would be able to enter the realm of the dead. But when they got to the entrance, an angel greeted them, and invited them to step inside and look. And the angel instructed them to tell Peter and the disciples to go to Galilee.

Mark refers to the two men who experienced the hospitality of Jesus on the road to Emmaus (see below), but he does not tell that whole story.

Mark says that Jesus met the apostles "at table" (the locus of hospitality) in Galilee (where native-born and strangers are intermingled), and that their work is extended from Galilee to "the whole world," (which is mostly strangers, until strangerdom shall pass away).

Luke, chapter 24

Luke's Gospel has the wonderful story of the Lord speaking to two men on the road to Emmaus. Several notes about hospitality in the story.

First, it is apparently not true that the people whom Jesus met in Judea and Galilee were more fortunate than we are today. They could meet him face to face and not recognize him. And so can we. This is a good reason to be habitually, consistently, and obediently hospitable.

Second, it is another story about the Lord meeting people who offer some hospitality, hospitality which he turns on its head. That is, they offer a little hospitality; he responds with overflowing gifts, eternally abundant.

Third, the chance meeting on the road resembled the Mass today. In fact, was it the first celebration of the Mass, the first time after the Last Supper? It had two parts: exploring Scripture, feeding their souls which burned within, and then breaking the bread together. "While he was with them at table, he took bread, said the blessing, broke it, and gave it to them. With that their eyes were opened and they recognized him" (Lk 24:30-31).

Fourth, when they followed Jesus on his way to Jerusalem, they "were hoping that he would be the one to redeem Israel." They were looking for the savior of Israel, and found him – but not until they recognized him as the Lord who offers hospitality.

Besides the Emmaus story, there is another complex example of hospitality in Luke's post-resurrection account. It's about Jesus calming the apostles and showing that he is human by eating some fish. But perhaps there is much more to the incident. Perhaps it is parallel to the pair of incidents in which Jesus multiplied loaves and fishes and then walked on the water (Mt 14 and Mk 6), and to incidents in the Exodus.

Matthew and Mark both recount the story of Jesus taking a few loaves of bread and a few fish, blessing them, distributing them – and feeding thousands. Both Gospels follow that incident immediately with the story of Jesus walking on the water. When the apostles saw him they were terrified, and thought they saw a ghost. He got in the boat, and told them not to be afraid. Didn't they understand the meaning of feeding five thousand?

The connection between walking on the water and feeding thousands is not obvious; but once Jesus made the point, we can figure it out. When he fed thousands miraculously, he was identifying himself as the same God who fed the Israelites in the desert with manna from heaven. That same God also parted the Red Sea so the Israelites could walk though dry-shod. He fed them in the desert, and he saved them from slavery.

In Luke's story account of events after the resurrection, Jesus met his followers in a room where they were gathered. They were terrified, and thought that they were seeing a ghost. When they saw him, he was not walking on water; he was walking back from death to life. He was not freeing them from slavery to the Egyptians; he was freeing them from slavery to death and the fear of death.

While the apostles were still wrestling with belief, Jesus asked them to provide a small bit of hospitality to him; he asked if they had anything to eat. They gave him a piece of fish, and he ate it. There is no indication that this was a shared meal; he ate it in front of them, and apparently they watched. When he fed thousands, he fed them so they would know he was God. This time, they feed him, so that they would know he is a man. Hospitality is partly about nourishment; but more importantly, it is about coming to know and understand the person whom you encounter. That is true with Moses in the desert, and then when Jesus feeds the thousands, and now when the apostles feed Jesus.

It is noteworthy that when the apostles were upset and afraid, Jesus calmed them down, partly by letting them see him eating like any other man, but also – perhaps – by giving them a way to serve. When we serve, we hope that we help the person whom we serve. But our service to someone else is a great benefit to us as well. The person who serves gets more from the encounter than the person served.

John, chapters 20-21

In John's Gospel, there is another pair of stories about water and bread, recalling the time when Jesus fed thousands and then walked on the water. John records that after the resurrection, Jesus appeared to the disciples repeatedly. The third time, they were out fishing, unsuccessfully. Jesus called out to them from the shore, telling them to try again, casting their net to the right. They caught so many that they were unable to pull the net in, at which point Peter recognized the Lord and jumped out of the boat. He didn't walk on the water, as he had once before, briefly (Mt 14: 24-33). This time, Peter's leap is natural not miraculous, enthusiastic not challenging, successful because the water was shallow and the shore was close, and tender. Again, the water was a delight, not an obstacle.

On shore, Jesus provided hospitality, giving them a breakfast of fish and bread. There was nothing overtly miraculous about it, except perhaps the size of the catch. Still, it was joyful. And again, it identified the Lord – not as divine, which the previous miracle had shown – but as human, as a hospitable Lord.

During his public ministry, Jesus explained something about himself by walking on water and multiplying loaves and fish. After the resurrection, he explains something else about himself, hanging out by the edge of the water and cooking up a completely normal breakfast. On both occasions, he explained himself amidst hospitality.

After breakfast, Jesus asked Peter three times, "Do you love me?" This matches the events after the Last Supper, when Jesus predicted accurately that Peter would deny him three times before the cock crowed in the morning. Peter responded to the question, three times, "Lord, you know that I love you." And three times, Jesus directed him to be hospitable: "Feed my lambs … tend my sheep … feed my sheep."

Peter's love was real, but imperfect. When Jesus had saved him, forgiven him, and healed him, he then challenged him to act in love – and more specifically, to be hospitable. Peter was chosen to lead, but not in pomp and power. The hallmark of his leadership was to be service and hospitality.

Chapter 19: Hospitality fills our prayer

The Lord is gentle but persistent. He will respond to our persistent prayers, because our persistent prayers are a fruit of his persistence. He knocks daily, and we open occasionally.

Jesus is the stranger in our prayer, as in our life – not always, but often.

It's odd and delightful that when Jesus appeared to his disciples after the resurrection, they didn't always recognize him. When he appeared to Mary Magdalen, she thought he was the gardener, until he spoke her name. When he appeared to the two men on the road to Emmaus, they didn't recognize him during a long conversation, although their hearts were on fire; they caught on only when he broke the bread. When he appeared by the side of the lake where they were fishing, they knew who he was, and yet it eased their minds when he ate something with them.

Throughout Scripture, and throughout our lives, God startles us. He loves us, and we respond with imperfect love. But he stretches us: he is unpredictable. He appears, repeatedly, as a total stranger – even to his closest disciples. Hospitality to strangers is an imitation of his love, a participation in his immense and overflowing love – but it is also plain prudence. Who is this guy knocking on my door?

He comes as a stranger, and so we must be alert. And so this book, this exploration of hospitality in the New Testament, is a success if Christians, especially Catholics, hear a call to hospitality when we:

1. read Scripture, or
2. go to Mass, or
3. pray the Divine Office with the Church, or
4. pray the Rosary, or
5. pray the Divine Mercy Chaplet.

This whole volume has been about finding the Lord in Scripture: the theme of hospitality is pervasive and once you see it, you can't un-see it, nor miss it. If hospitality pervades Scripture, then of course you will also see it all through the celebration of the Mass – in the readings, and throughout the liturgy of the

Eucharist. But also, hospitality shines through all the prayer of the Catholic Church.

Divine Office

The Divine Office, or Liturgy of the Hours, is a cycle of readings and prayers that monks sang together 15 centuries ago, and that men and women in various forms of religious life have prayed since. The "hours" in the title refers to the determination to build a life of prayer that includes regularly scheduled times of formal and focused prayer throughout each day, at specific hours. In ancient monastic prayer, the "hours" included dawn, then the first, third, sixth, and ninth hours (approximately 7 AM, 9 AM, noon, and 3 PM), then evening, then nightfall. The "office" refers to a responsibility or work, not a place. Each week, monks and others praying the Divine Office would sing or chant all 150 psalms, along with other readings and prayers, with times of silence and meditation. Today, the structure is looser, and the cycle to complete all the psalms is longer – reading all 150 every four weeks, instead of every single week. The three major hours – morning prayer, evening prayer, and night prayer – all include canticles or songs besides the Psalms, taken from Scripture.

That's background. The point is: the three canticles that are part of daily prayer for all who pray the Divine Office – the *Benedictus*, the *Magnificat*, and the *Nunc Dimittis* – all include references to hospitality.

The *Benedictus* is part of morning prayer every day in the Divine Office. It's a burst of joy, the words of Zechariah when his son was born and his own lips were finally released after months of silence. "Blessed," Zechariah erupts (*Benedictus* in Latin), "Blessed be the Lord, the God of Israel, for he has come to his people and set them free!" The canticle begins and ends with God breaking into our lives as a determined visitor, come to set us free. This is about hospitality and salvation, both. But it is easy to skip past the image at the beginning, to miss it completely. The text says that God "has (1) come to his people and (2) set them free." The word here for "come" (*episkeptomai*) is pro-active and determined, almost violent. It is the same word that shows up at the end of the canticle: "The dawn from on high shall (1) break upon us [rays of light stabbing through the forest, everywhere, irresistible and joyful and triumphant], to shine on those who dwell in darkness and the shadow of death, and (2) to guide our feet into the way of peace [saving us from violence and death]."

The word *episkeptomai* that Luke uses to describe the Lord *coming*, and dawn of a new world *breaking in* on us, is the same word that Matthew uses in describing the Last Judgment – to *visit* the sick and *visit* the imprisoned. It's a word of immense power and determination!

When the dawn breaks in, you are invited to be host to the Light of the World. Do it! (See the comments on the infancy narrative in Luke, above.)

The *Magnificat* is part of evening prayer, or Vespers, every day in the Divine Office. It's a love song, like the Song of Songs. But while the Song of Songs is sometimes interpreted as an exchange between a man and a woman, and other times as an exchange between God and his people – sometimes this, sometimes that – the Magnificat is always both. It is a combination and distillation of the two – a young woman singing about the God who loves her.

The setting for the Magnificat is the Visitation, a mutually satisfactory visit at which it was not possible to figure out who was host, who was guest. One was an old woman, beyond childbearing, an *aqar* in Hebrew; the other a virgin, an *almah* in Hebrew. Neither expected to welcome a child, but both are pregnant, by God's grace. And they are delighted for each other!

The song includes a detail about Mary's beloved, whose name fills her with joy that overflows in song: "The hungry he has filled with good things; the rich he has sent away empty." It's easy to abuse that line, to take lessons from it that may not really be there. That is, I'm not sure we should race to identify her as a fiery anti-capitalist. But for sure, we can ask who is pleased to hear this about the God who loves Mary. Her song pleases people in need of help, who depend on the generosity and hospitality of God. It seems to refer to the same thought that appears at the beginning of the Beatitudes: "Blessed are the poor in spirit, for theirs is the kingdom of God."

Night prayer in the Divine Office always includes the *Nunc Dimittis* ("now you dismiss"), the canticle of Simeon: "Now, Master, you may let your servant go in peace, according to your word, for my eyes have seen your salvation, which you prepared in sight of all the peoples, a light for revelation to the Gentiles, and glory for your people Israel" (Lk 2: 29-32). It seems like an appropriate way to end a day.

Simeon was an old man who was at the temple in Jerusalem when Mary and Joseph came to present Jesus to the Lord, as prescribed by the Law of Moses. Simeon believed that he would see the "consolation of Israel" before he died. And when he saw this proud young couple with their newborn, he came over and took the baby in his arms, saying, "Now, Master, you may dismiss your servant in peace ... my eyes have seen your salvation." Sometimes, I suspect, people reciting this canticle only get as far as the dismissal bit: "Now, Lord, I am done with today, and you can dismiss me to sleep." But Simeon wasn't just saying he was ready for death! He said, I have seen something! He looked at a child, and stated, "I have seen!" Simeon was the voice of welcome when Jesus came to the temple of his ancestors, the temple built to honor his Father. Simeon wasn't just smiling when a cooing cute child came in; he saw something, and proclaimed it: "Here and now, history changes! Details to follow!" He saw something, proclaimed the outline of it, and took vibrant joy in it. His whole heart, his whole life, was wrapped around that child! When Jesus came into this world and came to his own, his own did not recognize him, nor welcome him, for the most part. But Simeon did! In this tiny person – a mere baby, probably a total stranger – Simeon saw salvation, and a light to the Gentiles, and the glory of Israel.

I was privileged to teach for a while in a yeshiva, part of the school's "secular" faculty. The people who built the yeshiva were Orthodox, from different countries in eastern Europe, struggling to snatch victory from Hitler and maintain the whole way of life that the Nazis sought to end. Russian and Polish customs are still alive in Maryland – alive and growing. Hitler is disgraced and dead; but the yeshiva, though displaced, is doing fine. The Jews won. In that wonderful school, one spring, the principal took us to see the building that the community had bought, where a new school would be. The building had been a public school in the dim past, but it had been abandoned years before. It was run down when the county vacated it, and had been damaged even more since then. Standing in a cold dank dark corridor – home to rats and bats, vultures and vandals, who left scattered scraps and piles of scats, voracious rapacious and beady-eyed in their secret recesses, shadowy things of silent horror – there – with broken floors and rotten stairs and charred beams – there – she raised both her arms wide and gestured at a scarred and graffiti-marked wall, and said proudly, "And here is the new library!" I burst out laughing, and she stared at me, surprised. I loved that tough, tough woman, whose family and friends had died in cold dank dark death camps. She didn't say what I could perhaps have said, "Here's where the new library will be, if everything works out." No: she said "is," present tense, unqualified. She lived in hope, in real and vibrant hope. "My eyes have seen …"

And so spoke Simeon, who saw glory for his own humbled nation, and light for all the strangers of the world.

The Rosary

Among Catholics, the Rosary is the most popular form of personal prayer, running parallel to the Mass and the Divine Office – building on the pinnacle of our worship together in the Mass, and the daily prayer of all religious communities. The Rosary is a mildly complex form of prayer, almost always including at least three levels of deliberate focused attention: (1) meditation on a list of specific incidents in the life of our Lord, and (2) intercessory prayer for various "intentions," and (3) five prayers that we repeat. The 20 mysteries and the five prayers include numerous references to hospitality.

The Mysteries of the Rosary

All of the Joyful Mysteries are about scenes in the life of the Lord that include an element of hospitality (explored above). #1, the Annunciation: The angel of the Lord is received hospitably by Mary. The visit ends in a new covenant, the first of the covenants made between God and a woman. The covenant recalls Mamre, and both covenants are – later, finally – sealed by the blood of the Lamb. #2, the Visitation: This was a complex visit, with Elizabeth offering hospitality to Mary, Mary taking the initiative to bring hospitality to Elizabeth, and John greeting the Lord – not with a bow but a leap. #3, the Birth of the Lord: The mystery of the incarnation was revealed promptly to the shepherds and kings, strangers. And Jesus, no stranger to the world, was nonetheless rejected as an unwelcome stranger. #4, the Presentation at the Temple: Simeon welcomes Jesus, and predicts that the Gentiles will welcome his light. #5, the Finding at the Temple: Jesus returns to his home in Nazareth, in "Galilee of the Gentiles," where Jews and strangers live side by side.

The Sorrowful Mysteries are not really about hospitality. Two of the Glorious Mysteries refer obliquely to hospitality: the Ascension and Assumption refer to the home where Jesus has prepared hospitality for us.

The Luminous Mysteries, like the Joyful, all touch on hospitality. #1, the Baptism of the Lord: John is the herald, whose job is to ensure that people know they should be ready to offer hospitality to the one who is coming next. #2, Cana: We remember the event, but not the bride, nor the groom. One of the guests contributed to the feast; Jesus came as a guest, but then transformed that wedding, and all marriages, because he was made welcome. #3, the Proclamation of the Gospel: In every part of his public ministry, Jesus taught and demonstrated hospitality. #4, the Transfiguration: Peter and James and John saw something similar to what Abraham saw at Mamre. Peter wanted to provide hospitality – to erect tents for Jesus, Moses and Elijah – but a voice from the cloud instructing them to get directly to the heart of hospitality: listen! #5, the Eucharist: the Last Supper recalls the Passover, but also the First Feast at Mamre.

The Repeated Prayers of the Rosary

Each of the five fixed and repeated prayers includes some invitation to think about hospitality.

First: The *Sign of the Cross* points toward salvation and hospitality. It includes, in the gesture sketching a cross, a brief reminder that our salvation depends on the Lord. While our hands do one thing, our words do the other: the words are a brief reminder that the heart of our lives is the Lord who has revealed himself as a Triune God. Perhaps the best known image of the

Trinity is Andrei Rublev's icon of the Trinity, portrayed as the three strangers visiting Abraham at Mamre. One revealing ray of brilliant light from the heart of the Triune God is hospitality: the Father focused on the Son forever, the Son focused on the Father forever, the two joined into one by the work of the Holy Spirit forever.

Second: The *Our Father* includes two petitions on behalf of mankind: feed us and forgive us. These two petitions in the prayer that Jesus taught match the Exodus, when God freed his people from Egypt and then fed them in the desert.

Third: The *Hail Mary* refers to two tremendous instances of hospitality. The beginning of the prayer is the words of the angel who breaks into Mary's life like the dawn, and finds her perfectly receptive. The second sentence is Elizabeth's greeting to Mary, when the two shared hospitality. And the prayer ends with a request that Mary help us at the hour of death, that we might find hospitality in heaven.

Fourth: The Glory Be (or Doxology) refers again to the life of the Trinity, a mystery of hospitality forever. The Father and the Son are joined together as one, eternally, in a union that we may glimpse in marriage, and may glimpse in the host-guest relationship.

Fifth: The Rosary end with the Salve Regina, which identifies us as a banished people, living in a valley of tears, and asks that Mary be an advocate for us, ending our exile and bringing us to know her son forever.

A Note on the Divine Mercy Chaplet

The payer taught by St. Faustina is brief: "For the sake of his sorrowful passion, have mercy on us and on the whole world." The worlds are about the crucifixion and death of the Lord. This is a Good Friday prayer, not a Holy Thursday prayer. But often, perhaps all the time, when people pray the Divine Mercy Chaplet, they have an intention, a specific request, in mind. We go to the Lord asking for something, depending on his generosity. Petitioners are confident that he will receive us hospitably, and listen to us. The words of the prayer are about contrition, asking for salvation. But the intent of the prayer includes releasing God's generosity into the world in some way.

We pray for mercy – for us, and for world – and the person who prays is a beggar before the source of all good things. But intercessory prayer is not purely passive. In some way, in the economy of grace, the generosity of God includes the person who intercedes as a conduit of grace, not merely a passive recipient. To emphasize this, the Church named St. Therese of Lisieux a "Doctor" of the Church. The prayers of this young cloistered nun are understood to be active and transformative.

Both activists and contemplatives take Mary as a model. In her, the word was made flesh: just so, activists struggle to hear and grasp the Lord's prophetic word, and then bring it alive and thriving into the world of time and space. But also, she listened and pondered: just so, contemplatives sit at the feet of the Lord, listening to the Lord with admiration and love. Hospitality includes both doing what we can for those who come into our lives, and listening to the Lord in and through our guests.

Chapter 20: Beacon on a hill

You are the salt of the earth. But if salt loses its taste, with what can it be seasoned? It is no longer good for anything but to be thrown out and trampled underfoot. You are the light of the world. A city set on a mountain cannot be hidden. (Mt 5:13-14)

So what do we learn from the New Testament about immigration?

First, the abundant and forceful teaching throughout the Old Testament is not in any way diminished in the New Testament. Welcoming strangers matters. God is not a safe pet; he created the universe and we know him only because he invited us to know him, and he reveals himself. And when he reveals himself to us, he stretches us – not always, but often. He is our Father, but he is also Other. It is not possible to dismiss the Other – or others, or strangers – and yet find God.

Second, there are indeed some changes in the way hospitality to strangers is presented in the New Testament, compared to the Old Testament. The Scriptures written in an occupied nation differ in some superficial ways from Scripture written in a nation struggling to gain or maintain proud independence. One can argue that there is a sharper emphasis on personal one-on-one hospitality in the New Testament. But even if that's true, the shift in emphasis is in no way a replacement for the social concerns found more frequently in the Old Testament. The teaching about personal responsibility emphasizes that even if the nation of Israel or the people of God cannot offer hospitality corporately, individuals still can and should. Hospitality is a duty that remains even if the state cannot fulfill its proper duties.

Social action to provide hospitality to immigrants was standard in the Old Testament. It was perhaps somewhat diminished in the early Church. But the teaching of all Scripture, including the teaching of Jesus, points toward it. The "social gospel" of the past 150 years was not in any way a departure from the teaching of the New Testament; it is an on-going reaction to the signs of the times, based squarely on Scripture and Tradition.

Hospitality is a ray of light direct from the glowing heart of the Trinity. It's not the fullness of the Gospel; it is a single ray, like chastity or martyrdom. It bursts forth from God, and shines throughout creation.

In the Sermon on the Mount, Jesus says of the Church that we are to be a light on a hill. If the structure on a hilltop has strong stone walls that keep others out, that's a castle, not a church. A light on a hill is a sign of hope, offering the possibility of escape from the shadow of darkness, the valley of tears. It is a heart-born beacon that beckons, not cold stone that rebukes the broken heart.

When Jesus asks of us that we become a light on a hill, some find that to be an invitation to arrogance. It is perhaps useful to note that the call to be a light goes with a call to be salt. Salt is a symbol of hospitality. But when you find salt – without food, and without guests, just salt by itself – you have been cursed. Salt, by itself, will shrivel you, make you ugly, and kill you. It's best to shake it loose, spread it around, and share it.

The light-heartedness of hospitality shines throughout creation, and throughout Scripture. Once you see it, you cannot un-see it. And once you start to notice it, you find it glowing everywhere that God has been.

Exploring the abundant teaching on hospitality in the New Testament, even superficially, I found three patterns worth noting. First, it is extraordinarily instructive to compare examples of hospitality. Second, it is common for the host and guest to switch roles – not in confusion but in unity. Third, I was startled by how often hospitality is paired with forgiveness and salvation.

Comparing instances of hospitality

The prototype of hospitality is described carefully in the story of Abraham welcoming guests at Mamre, the First Feast in Scripture. But to understand that story, it is helpful to compare it to the next chapter in Genesis, the story of Sodom. There are many significant parallels: bowing, water for the guests' feet, invitation to rest, bread, feast, wife in trouble, the growing intensity and depth of the story, business after dinner, intercessory prayer, the immensity of God's gifts. Noting the parallels, and looking for them in the accounts of the Last Supper, is immensely instructive: Jesus bent to the floor as a servant, washing his guests' feet himself, the bread of life, the eternal banquet, Judas in trouble, the intensity of the story, serious business after dinner, intercessory prayer in the Garden of Gethsemane, and unimaginably glorious gifts.

But then, it is also worthwhile contrasting these events with other examples of hospitality. When Jesus met the woman at the well, that event included: banter (instead of immediate hospitality), water, a woman in trouble, rapidly accumulating intensity and depth, spillover to community, and huge gifts from a generous Lord and forgiving savior.

When the angel visited Mary, there is no mention of bowing or water or a feast, but there is clear mutual respect. Sarah laughing at the impossible at Mamre is matched in Luke by Joseph doubting; both Sarah and Joseph were pulled into the plans after their initial hesitations. The promise to Abraham took years to get clear – one son, two grandsons, then an explosion of fertile great-grandsons. It was 30 years before the promise to Mary was made manifest to the world, and 20 centuries later we are still figuring it out.

Host-Guest Unity

One of the great joys of hospitality is the possibility or likelihood that hospitality will become a living image of the Trinity, in the sense that the two become one, and the relationship develops in such that you can't tell who is host and who is guest. Examples:

> 1. When Abraham welcomed three guests, he began as host. But before the end of the day, it was clear that his guests were God and two angels – who set the agenda and poured out gifts.
> 2. When Lot welcomed two guests, he began as host. But before the end of the night, it was clear that his guests were angels – who set the agenda and protected his life.
> 3. When Elijah visited the widow of Zarephath, she was hostess initially. But within a few hours, it was clear that he was a prophet. He set the agenda, and made sure she had food and protection for months.

4. At Cana, Jesus came as a guest. But he provided the wine, the joy of the event.

5. When Jesus spoke with the Roman centurion about healing his servant, the centurion understood clearly who would benefit if Jesus came to visit. This guest was far above the host. We recall that at every Mass: when we offer Jesus hospitality in our hearts, and he comes gently, but as Lord.

6. When Jesus met the woman at the well, he asked her to provide hospitality – specifically, water. He asked her to be hostess. But soon, it was clear that he was gift-giver. He drew her out of degradation in her community, and gave her the gift of eternal life.

7. At the Transfiguration, Peter wanted to provide hospitality. He didn't know what he was talking about. But in the Ascension, Jesus leaves, promising to prepare a place for his followers, including Peter. Jesus will provide the hospitality that Peter wanted to provide.

8. In general: "Do not neglect hospitality, for through it some have unknowingly entertained angels" (Heb 13:2).

Pairing salvation and hospitality

The teaching of Moses has a persistent pair. He named his two sons Gershom and Eliezer, referring to hospitality to strangers and God's action to save his people. When he recalled the lessons from the Exodus, he repeated many times that we should remember that we were slaves until God freed us, and we should welcome strangers because we remember that we too once were strangers in a strange land. The Israelites went across the Red Sea out of slavery into freedom, then God fed them in the desert with manna. Moses repeats it over and over, in many ways: God saved us and fed us.

Jesus picked up Moses' thought. He expected the disciples to understand that his hospitality feeding 5,000 people meant that he could also lead them across the water (of Galilee, or baptism) to freedom. He seemed to say that *of course* these two ideas are linked. (Oh.)

Zechariah proclaimed that God has "come to his people and set them free." That's easy to miss, but it was indeed two overlapping but separable acts, Christmas and Easter, hospitality and salvation.

Jesus is Lord and Savior. But note: his lordship is more a matter of hosting a feast than of pomp and power.

The Lord taught us to pray, asking the Father to give us our daily bread, and forgive us.

On the cross, Jesus spoke to his companion in suffering and death, promising that he would be in paradise that day: salvation and welcome combined.

Abraham was the type of hospitality at Mamre, and sacrifice at Moriah. Jesus imitated his father Abraham, with the Passover Feast on Holy Thursday, followed by his saving act of suffering and death on Good Friday.

When he spoke with the Samaritan woman at the well, he asked for hospitality, then gave her living water – salvation and hospitality.

When Jesus was born, he was called two names – Jesus, which refers to salvation, and Emmanuel, which refers to hospitality.

Thomas Aquinas, commenting on the Lord's act of washing his disciples' feet, sees this act of hospitality as a symbol of forgiveness.

After the resurrection, when Jesus forgave Peter for betraying him three times, he then instructed him three times to provide hospitality: "Feed my sheep."

Following the bishops

In their powerful document about welcoming immigrants, "Strangers No Longer," the American and Mexican bishops sketched the Scriptural basis for their teaching. They used 15 passages from Genesis, Exodus, Leviticus, Deuteronomy, Matthew, Acts, and Ephesians (Gn 12:1, Gn 37:45, Ex 23:9, Lv 19:9-10, Lv 19:33, Dt 10:17-19, Dt 14:28-29, Mt 2:15, Mt 25:31, Mt 25:35, Mt 25:35-36, Mt 25:40, Mt 28:16-20, Acts 2:1-21, Eph 2:17-20).

To ground their words, they explored Abraham's call and his hospitality to three strangers, and Joseph's experience going into Egypt as a slave. They reviewed God's liberation of his people, and his commandments regarding strangers. They noted that the commands about care for strangers were personal exhortations, but also structured into the laws. They recalled the Holy Family's flight into Egypt. The noted the Lord's description of the Last Judgment. And they pondered the call to unite all peoples and races in one family of God.

I am confident that my work corresponds to their teaching. My purpose in this volume has been more limited than theirs: I set out to show that the Lord's words about the Last Judgment complete and solidify teaching all through the Old Testament, and that there is abundant and urgent teaching about hospitality all through Scripture. To make my argument in the Old Testament, I used 21 passages. In this volume, to show that the teaching didn't slide into oblivion in the New Testament, I looked at over 60 passages.

Once you see the teaching, you find it everywhere. The bishops pointed the way. I scratched the surface. Alert readers will see far, far more examples.

"Come, you who are blessed by my Father. Inherit the kingdom prepared for you from the foundation of the world. For I was ... a stranger and you welcomed me."

"When ...?"

"Amen, I say to you, whatever you did for one of these least brothers of mine, you did for me."

About the Author

John Cavanaugh-O'Keefe is best known for his work as an activist, building the nonviolent branch of the pro-life movement. He has been called "Father of the Rescue Movement" by *Time*, *NY Times Magazine*, Joan Andrews, Joe Scheidler, and others. James Risen (*LA Times*) and Judy L. Thomas's (*KC Star*) history of the rescue movement, *Wrath of Angels*, also uses this title. Cavanaugh-O'Keefe notes that the title is odd, because the real leaders of the rescue movement are mostly women, including Jeanne Miller Gaetano, Dr. Lucy Hancock, Jo McGowan, Joan Andrews, Juli Loesch Wiley, Kathie O'Keefe, ChristyAnne Collins, Monica Migliorino Miller, and others. But his writing – especially *No Cheap Solutions* and *Emmanuel, Solidarity: God's Act, Our Response* – influenced activists in the US, Canada, Mexico, Brazil, all over Europe, Philippines, Korea, and Australia.

Cavanaugh-O'Keefe has been arrested 39 times for civil disobedience. He was in the first group that was jailed for pro-life nonviolent action (in Connecticut, 1978). He was among the three organizers of the "We Will Stand Up" campaign, the most successful event of the rescue movement, closing all the abortion clinics in eight of the nine cities that Pope John Paul II visited in 1987. He initiated the Tobit Project, taking bodies out of dumpsters in the Washington area and providing respectful burials.

He has written extensively about eugenics and population control; see especially The Roots of Racism and Abortion. He participated in efforts to resist the population reduction campaigns, particularly in South Africa under the apartheid government, and in Bangladesh; see especially "Deadly Neocolonialism." He supported the work of the Information Project for Africa, which brought feminists and pro-lifers together to resist coercive depopulation measures at the UN population conference in Cairo.

He has written about eugenics and human cloning. When President Clinton established his National Bioethics Advisory Commission (NBAC), Cavanaugh-O'Keefe helped form a grass-roots commission in response – the American Bioethics Advisory Commission (ABAC), and served as the ABAC's first executive director. The first policy question that the Clinton's NBAC addressed was human cloning, and their report has sections on eugenics and dignity that were written in response to input from Cavanaugh-O'Keefe. When the NBAC completed their work and published a report supporting human cloning as long as the clone is destroyed in the embryonic or fetal stage and never reaches adulthood, the ABAC worked with the United States Conference of Catholic Bishops against this "clone-and-kill" proposal.

He has written about eugenics and immigration; see especially his study of Scriptural teaching about the mandate to welcome strangers in *Sign of the Crossing* and *Welcome Date TBD*.

Throughout his life, Cavanaugh-O'Keefe has worked to cross-fertilize, and to maintain civil dialogue with opponents. He worked with Pro-lifers for Survival, as editor of the group's publication, P.S. This ambitious organization brought peace activists and pro-life activists together; their challenging work was later taken over by Cardinal Bernardin. Cavanaugh-O'Keefe was proud to be invited to contribute to the *Women's Studies Encyclopedia*; crossing an ideological divide, he wrote their article explaining the pro-life movement. He worked with a common ground group in the Washington area, bringing pro-life and pro-choice activists together – not to find compromises, but to encourage respect and understanding.

In 2012, Cavanaugh-O'Keefe began working to strengthen the unity of the Catholic Church by encouraging pro-life and pro-family activists to re-consider their positions on immigration, and encouraging pro-immigration activists to reconsider their positions on life and marriage. See www.SignoftheCrossing.org.

He and his wife live in Maryland, where they raised six children and now enjoy ten (plus) grandchildren.

Made in the USA
Middletown, DE
10 May 2019